P9-DMX-188

A Woman's Guide to Financial Peace of Mind

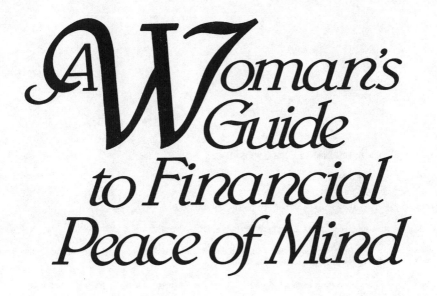

Ron and Judy Blue

PUBLISHING

Pomona, California

A WOMAN'S GUIDE TO FINANCIAL PEACE OF MIND

Copyright © 1991 by Ron and Judy Blue
  ISBN 1-56179-026-5

Published by Focus on the Family Publishing, Pomona, California 91799.

Distributed in the United States and Canada by Word Books, Dallas, Texas.

Unless otherwise noted, Scripture quotations are from the Holy Bible, New International Version, copyright © 1973, 1978, 1984 by the International Bible Society.

Editor: Larry K. Weeden
Art Director: Timothy Jones
Cover Illustrator: Lee Christiansen

Printed in the United States of America

Contents

Acknowledgments

Many people deserve our thanks and appreciation for playing a part in the creation of this book. Our children, while teasing us unmercifully to keep us humble (which they see as their mission in life), have been most understanding of the time demanded of us to meet our deadlines. They are truly precious gifts from God.

We've also been blessed with a supportive and encouraging staff at Ronald Blue & Co. Zoe Custer, Ron's secretary, has once again demonstrated a patience and perseverance without which this book could not have been completed on time. She has prodded gently and kept us on track, for which we're grateful.

Jane Jackson was extremely flexible as typing schedules were changed, changed again, ignored and then set with impossible deadlines. Her gracious acceptance of all the changes made finishing the book a much easier task than we could have hoped.

Wendy Morgan and Kathy Cook, both from our staff, read the first draft, made some outstanding suggestions for changes and in the process gave us encouragement to continue. Their contribution to the readability of the book is gratefully acknowledged.

Scott Houser and Curt Knorr, also from our staff, made major contributions as well. Scott drafted chapter 16 (on health insurance), and Curt designed all the charts, making the data easier to understand.

This book would not have come to fruition without the kind and insightful direction of Larry Weeden, our editor. The staff at Focus on the Family represent all that is good in the American Christian community. Their contribution to the development of the family will be eternally acknowledged.

The faithful Christian women we have had the privilege of meeting over the past years are the real inspiration for this book. So many are managing well the resources God has entrusted to them, and we applaud their efforts. For those of you who are struggling financially, please know it is never our intention to criticize. Rather, we want to offer constructive help so that in this area as in all others, you can work with our Lord for the furtherance of His kingdom and find Him sufficient for all your needs.

Introduction

We have to start with a confession: We don't enjoy writing books. There's a tremendous risk in holding yourself out as an expert in anything, because knowledge is no guarantee of success. Also, the process of writing books can be arduous and is not something we particularly like. As we've gotten into this project, however, we've found ourselves growing more excited than we've been about any other book we've done.

Ron was trained as an accountant, spent three years in full-time ministry, and in the last eleven years has combined his technical background with his ministry desire in a financial planning practice primarily serving Christians. As we have gathered information to write this book, he has realized that all he's been doing over the last fifteen years is coming together in this project.

We're excited about writing specifically to women because we've found that they're usually more teachable than men and that men can be reached better through women than any other way. Many men are confident of their ability to manage money but actually have very little training or skill. And while the financial problems and decisions of life are not too much different for men and women, the way those challenges are viewed, and the process of making decisions, can be considerably different for the two sexes.

Our insights into those differences and the counsel we offer here on the financial seasons of a woman's life come from several sources: our personal experience as a family with three daughters and two sons; Ron's observations drawn from speaking, teaching and public ministry; observations drawn from the more than two thousand clients Ron's firm has serviced over the years; and the results of a nationwide survey conducted for this book by a group of marketing students at Azusa Pacific University.

Those experiences and observations lead us to the following broad conclusions. First, women tend to be security-oriented in their attitude toward money, whereas men tend to be more motivated by a desire for significance. It's common, for example, for a husband to want to invest in the stock market while the wife wants to pay off the home mortgage. The man, even though he's godly, is driven more by the need to build something of significance than by the desire to provide short-term security for his family. His wife, on the other hand, is far more driven to provide immediate security.

That's a major difference in our own relationship. Fortunately, we have learned how to communicate and balance each other out. Left to his own devices, Ron would probably risk everything on a good-looking investment. Judy, on the other hand, would probably risk nothing. Neither tendency is right or wrong—they're just different.

Second, women tend to be more short-term and detail-oriented in their thinking and decision making, whereas men tend to be more long-term in their thinking and like to look at the "big picture." A good example of this basic difference is that if a couple were going to another home for dinner, the woman would be very interested in how the table was set, whereas the man would be more apt to look at the size and value of the house.

Third, women tend to be more intuitive in their decision making, whereas men tend to be more logical. That *doesn't* mean men make better decisions. In fact, research shows that given the same set of facts, women's decisions tend to be as good as—if not better than—men's.

What We Want to Accomplish

We have four objectives in writing this book. First, we want it to be scripturally sound, and we've been careful to make sure it is. Second, we want to communicate clearly about financial concepts that are often misunderstood. Third, we want to be very practical and helpful. Fourth, we want to challenge you to a greater commitment to Jesus Christ through better stewardship of the financial resources He entrusts to you.

Our great challenge is to provide practical guidance for an audience of unique individuals, yet not overwhelm you with information so that the book becomes useless. We've worked hard to meet that challenge.

We believe there's a great need for a book such as this, because women have a lot of money management responsibility but little practical training. Women are also called upon to communicate with their husbands in this vital area, yet men may not feel comfortable discussing it, and they may also think their wives won't understand the terms and concepts if they do talk about it. And like it or not, most women will end up managing *all* the household finances some day, as seven out of ten married women will eventually face widowhood.

The seasons-of-life approach in part 2 of this book allows you to focus on the specific challenges you're probably facing at your current stage in life. It will also give you an overall framework for money management that will help you to handle money successfully throughout your life.

These seasons of life are determined by age, marital status, age of children and income level. We identify them as follows:

1. *The young single.* This is a person from the ages of twenty to thirty, and she would be differentiated from the single parent and the career single.

2. *The young married.* This person could be any age from about twenty to forty.

3. *The mother of young children.* Typically this person has been married from three to ten years.

4. *The mother of teen and college-age children.* This woman has usually been married for between fourteen and twenty-five years.

5. *The empty nest.* A woman at this stage has been married from twenty to thirty years and is typically forty to sixty years old.

6. *Retirement.* This normally comes sometime between the ages of fifty-five and seventy-five.

7. *Widowhood.* This generally occurs at the empty nest age or later.

8. *Single parent.* A woman can find herself in this position at any time after children are born.

9. *Career single.* This woman is unmarried and between the ages of thirty and retirement.

Before turning to the specifics of the different stages of life, however, we lay a foundation of basic financial principles in part 1. That foundation is anchored by four cornerstones of successful money management that will never change regardless of your season of life. Applying them continually is the key to financial success in any season. What follows is a brief summary of the four cornerstones.

The Cornerstones of Success

Cornerstone #1: A growing relationship with God

This is the chief cornerstone. You can have millions of dollars and still not be financially successful if you're not walking with the Lord and allowing His Word to direct all your ways, including your use of money. The Bible has much to say about money and money management, and it has everything to say about how to live. A proper understanding of biblical truths applied to your unique financial situation is ongoing and essential to ultimate financial success.

Cornerstone #2: Sound financial principles

Successful financial principles will always transcend financial situations. In other words, a sound principle doesn't become unsound just because circumstances change. If it's applied correctly, it will always work. Good money management requires the continuous application of such well-proven principles throughout life.

Cornerstone #3: Basic financial skills

Think of money management skills as the tools that allow you to apply the principles in your life. These skills are learned by consistent and repetitive practice. Just a few basic skills, used as needed, will bring you success.

Cornerstone #4: Financial planning

Financial planning is an ongoing process rather than a one-time event. Applying our five-step process to your unique situation will ensure that you are continually on track to avoid problems and make good financial decisions. Don't worry—the process isn't as complicated or difficult as you might think.

How to Use This Book

This book can be used in several ways. Reading just the first four chapters will give you a basic understanding of sound money management from a Christian perspective. That understanding will help reduce the confusion that comes from advertising, peer groups and the day-to-day concerns that are the result of living in a media-oriented society. Such a framework will help you evaluate information and apply it to your specific situation.

Realizing there are different seasons of life, with different problems and decisions to be made during them, will also reduce some of the fear and frustration that come from the continual need to make financial decisions. There is comfort in knowing, regarding your present concerns, that "this too will pass." Of course, more decisions face you down the road, but having some idea of what you might confront in the next season of life can better prepare you to deal with it.

Our hope is that this book will not only be helpful to you, but also to your husband or whoever else helps you make financial decisions. We've included information on investments, financial planning, insurance, major decisions to be made and useful tools. We hope this makes it a well-used reference book.

Not all questions will be answered by this book, of course, and we hope you'll do further study on topics of personal interest. We've included references to a number of other resources that should be useful to you.

We recommend the following approach to using this book. First, read part 1 to get an overview of the basics of money management. Second, read the chapter dealing with your current season of life. Also read the chapter preceding it and the one describing the season of life you'll be in next. In that way you'll get a good perspective on where you are, where you've been and where you're going—the proper context for understanding your current stage of life. Third, turn to the final four chapters, which are detailed, reference-type chapters, as you have specific need of them.

How This Book Was Written

You may wonder how we worked together in writing this book when Ron is the so-called expert in the family. It's true that Judy is not a trained financial adviser, but we've been married for more than twenty-six years, have raised five children and have had many ups and downs in all areas of our lives. Over the years, Ron has grown to respect her counsel immeasurably. She is his most-trusted confidante. Her ability to add wisdom to family financial decisions is essential; many times, her judgments have been better than Ron's.

Therefore, this book has been written very much by both of us, even though most of the examples come naturally from Ron's professional experiences. Judy has the ability to review what is written in terms of its applicability to most women. She has already been through many of the seasons of life herself and so can identify with the needs at each stage. Thus, besides providing a great deal of input at the beginning, she has also read and given feedback on every word written. To whatever extent this book is readable and meets women's needs, she deserves much of the credit.

Challenge

As you look in this book at what you need to know and do to manage your money wisely, our concern is that you not feel overwhelmed. We really want this book to be helpful rather than intimidating. It might give you some comfort to remember that common sense is generally right when it comes to money management.

Additionally, financial planning and money management are really not that difficult once they're properly understood. You don't need to be a Wall Street wizard or have an MBA hanging on the wall to handle money well.

Remember, too, that even though your problems or challenges may seem overwhelming, you only need to take one small step at a time. You begin where you are, not where you would like to be. It's a lot like eating an elephant: you do it one bite at a time. And the next small bite is the only one you have to focus on at a given moment. Once you finish it, you'll be ready for the next bite, and eventually the elephant will be gone.

We know from our own experience that God is faithful. The mere fact that you're reading this book indicates a desire on your part to do what's right. God in turn will do His part to provide what you need in the way of wisdom, counselors, understanding, financial resources and so on. Please understand that He may not meet your needs in the way you would expect or within the time frame you would like. But at some point you will be able to reflect and say, "Look at what God has done!"

CHAPTER ONE

Making Ends Meet

*M*ary was a stewardess on a cross-country flight Ron took recently. He had just boarded the plane when a flight attendant said over the intercom, "Would Ron Blue please ring the call button." He was a bit alarmed, not knowing why he was being paged. He pushed the call button, and a stewardess soon appeared to ask if he had ordered a special meal. He told her he had.

She then looked at him and hesitantly said, "Are you by any chance the Ron Blue who writes about money?"

He told her he had written a couple of books on the subject.

"My name is Mary," she said, "and I need to talk to you. My husband has read your books, and I have some questions. As soon as we've completed the meal service, I'll be back."

Because this was a flight from Atlanta to California, taking more than four and a half hours, Ron knew Mary would have plenty of time to air her complaints, and he was trapped.

It turned out she was not irate but frustrated, confused and concerned. One of her first comments was "It seems as if the more money we have, the more problems we have financially. Our worries only get bigger."

Mary's husband was a self-employed professional whose income, while very good, varied dramatically from month to month. They had been married eighteen years, were Christians, and had three children ages fourteen, eleven and ten. They really wanted to manage their money in a biblically correct way. Yet Mary told Ron that her fourteen-year-old son, who frequently made $100 or more per week baby-sitting and mowing lawns, seemed to have more money than she did.

"What would your greatest financial desire be?" Ron asked her.

"To be totally free from a mortgage," she answered immediately. "But that will only happen if our ship comes in someday."

As they chatted, Ron found out several other things about her. Her parents had earned enough to provide each of their children with all the necessities and most of their wants. As a result, managing money had never been important to Mary as a child or college student.

After she got married, her husband continued where her parents had left off by giving her money as she asked for it. Only recently, as their children got older and they experienced some financial stress, had she and her husband become serious about managing money. That was why he had purchased Ron's book, and they were now trying to institute the budgeting system outlined there.

Then Mary made a significant comment regarding women and money management: "My biggest problem in life is managing money. It causes more stress in my marriage relationship than anything else. I can handle raising children and being a wife as well as working as a flight attendant, but I can't handle the stress of managing money."

The Stress of Money Management

Mary is representative of the 60 percent of Christian women who work outside the home at least part-time, according to our survey. We believe what she said about the stress of managing money being greater than the multiple pressures of motherhood, marriage and career.

As we've talked with Christian women across the country, a multitude of common stresses and concerns have been revealed. For example, one woman said on behalf of many, "How do you keep from living month to month or paycheck to paycheck?"

"How can I be sure to have enough funds on hand if something happens to my husband?" asked another.

"What's the best way to get out of debt ASAP?" said a third.

"If we owe money to our parents and can't pay them back, should we be tithing?" asked another woman.

And one lady voiced the general anxiety felt by a lot of us: "What is the best financial protection for the future in our unstable world?"

Young single women face pressures of their own. We once asked our oldest daughter, who is twenty-four at the time of this writing, how her peer group would define financial success. She gave the best worldly definition of success we've heard. "My friends believe financial success is having whatever you want whenever you want it," she said.

The world has not only inadequately prepared those young women for responsible money management, but it also demands that they have all the material possessions their hearts desire whenever they want them. Such an attitude is obviously expensive to satisfy. Women who try to meet it are going to choose a high-income career, go deeply into debt, find a husband who will meet the need or all the above.

We're not saying that any woman who works outside the home is motivated by materialism, but we are saying that it's difficult to ignore the siren song of materialism in our culture. There is much confusion, fear and doubt when it comes to making financial decisions.

Those anxieties are probably never more intensified than in a new widow or a newly divorced woman, especially if she has children to raise.

An article about single mothers in the *Atlanta Journal & Constitution* (May 7, 1990) told of Mary Goodwin, a divorced woman who had found herself falling ever deeper into debt. To earn more money, for about a year she got up at around three every morning and delivered newspapers until seven. Then she showered, took her son to school and went to her regular job as a bookkeeper.

Despite all that effort, however, she could never get caught up. "There was no way that I could make enough money to pay off everything that was owed," she told the reporter. "You feel like you're drowning. Eventually, you can't take it anymore." In the end, she decided to file for bankruptcy, leaving behind thousands of dollars of debt.

Unfortunately, her experience of financial disaster is all too common for divorced mothers. The reasons range from increased expenses to inadequate or nonexistent child-support payments.

Divorce is faced by 50 percent of all women who marry and has its own set of financial problems (more about them in chap. 12). Widowhood, however, is faced by an even larger percentage of women—seven out of ten married women. A study we came across some time ago said that the average age of widows in America is fifty-two. So most women, at some point in their lives, will end up as the primary money manager of a household (if they weren't already). And most of them will have had very little training for the task.

Common Influences on Financial Thinking

Each woman is unique. But our experience and research indicate there are several common influences on women's thinking about money. One that makes a big difference is age. Younger women are concerned about furnishing a home and the cost of raising children. "How can you save for home improvements or a car when you have to keep paying for things that have broken down?" a mother asked us.

Most women, at some point in their lives, will end up as the primary money manager of a household (if they weren't already). And most of them will have had very little training for the task.

As the kids grow, women think about providing for college education. Older women tend to be far more concerned about building financial security than acquiring possessions. Most of the things they have they'll soon be getting rid of in one way or another. They're thinking along the lines of the woman who nervously asked us, "Will Social Security still be around when my husband and I retire?" The widowhood and retirement issues that concern older women are so far in the future for young women, however, that they aren't given a lot of thought.

Income level also has a big influence on financial concerns. When young couples are first beginning to buy the goods to set up a household, there is rarely

> *Communication about money is usually a good indicator of the quality of communication in all other areas of a marriage.*

enough income to meet all the apparent needs. What happens over time, however, is that even as income goes up, so do needs—perhaps even faster. The result is that older women who have high personal incomes or well-paid husbands still have significant financial concerns. "Why do we struggle so much when we're making $47,000 a year?" one woman asked us in all seriousness.

The stresses of the well-to-do wouldn't seem as critical to younger women compared to their own, but to older women with high incomes, more money doesn't mean fewer problems. As a matter of fact, more income brings more ways to spend money and therefore more decisions to be made.

A woman's relationship with her husband, be it good or bad, can also have a tremendous impact on her needs and views regarding money. (Imagine the outlook of the wife who told us, "My husband often seems unconcerned about his financial responsibility. I get the impression he really doesn't want to work.") Communication about money is usually a good indicator of the quality of communication in all other areas of a marriage. If the communication is good, money problems tend to be worked out well. Unfortunately, the opposite is also true.

Whether or not a woman works, how many children she has and the ages of those children further affect her financial needs and decisions. Those with young children have little time to even think about money, let alone the development of an investment plan, an estate plan or a long-range financial plan. As the children get older and become more self-sufficient, however, more time and energy are available to deal with money issues.

A woman's spiritual maturity will also affect her monetary thoughts and fears. As Christians, we can be totally secure in all areas of our lives. Many people do not experience that security, however, because they haven't learned how to trust God for their needs and the future.

Whether a woman has the ability to hire a financial adviser or tax preparer can certainly influence her decisions. A single woman who is just getting by tends to have many questions. The inability to hire an adviser may fuel her fears and frustrations. (That's *not* to say that hiring a financial adviser will solve all financial problems.)

The list could go on, but the point is that addressing the needs of women and finances is not simple. So many variables are involved that, in some cases, generalizations are of little help. We have tried to write this book with as few generalizations as possible, giving specific advice that will be helpful and practical wherever you are in your financial life.

Like any set of skills, however, successful money management has to be based on a sound foundation, with rock-solid cornerstones. So before we look at the seasons of life and the specific concerns of each, we turn in the next few chapters to those cornerstones that will anchor your financial future and make possible your peace of mind.

CHAPTER TWO

Cornerstones of Success
Part One

*T*he following letter is the most encouraging Ron has ever received in his ministry.

Dear Ron,

Last October I was in a local Christian bookstore...and came across your book *Master Your Money* on one of the shelves. In August, I had decided to free myself of a particular financial drain, and this book seemed like a good way to start doing things differently. We swallowed hard, primed the checkbook with one month's expenses and created a budget worksheet.

After seven months of following these principles, we've managed to do more with our money than in the last seventeen years of our marriage! We have more than doubled our giving to the Lord, which was the primary reason for changing things in the first place. We wondered how we could ever tithe and are now exceeding it! We set up long-term and short-term plans, and the Lord has blessed us. We bought the new house we wanted, the thought of which in the past created financial anxieties. We have no more than we did before, but being better

> stewards has made all the difference.
> We can't begin to express the joy we have found in applying
> these biblical principles to our financial management. We have
> shared these things with our friends...

Two sentences in that letter particularly caught our eyes as we read it: "We've more than doubled our giving to the Lord, which was the primary reason for changing things in the first place" and, very importantly, "We have no more than we did before, but being better stewards has made all the difference."

Jesus said in Matthew 7:24-27:

> Therefore everyone who hears these words of mine and puts
> them into practice is like a wise man who built his house on the
> rock. The rain came down, the streams rose, and the winds blew
> and beat against that house; yet it did not fall, because it had its
> foundation on the rock. But everyone who hears these words of
> mine and does not put them into practice is like a foolish man
> who built his house on sand. The rain came down, the streams
> rose, and the winds blew and beat against that house, and it fell
> with a great crash.

The basics of money management are biblically sound, and when they're applied to an individual's unique financial situation, that person is like the one who builds a house on rock. Adversity may come, but catastrophe does not. The result can be as the couple said: "We can't begin to express the joy we found in applying these biblical principles to our financial management."

Practicing the cornerstones we're going to talk about in this chapter and the next will set you apart as someone different. Our culture has it all wrong in measuring success. The true measure is found in Matthew 25:21: "His master replied, 'Well done, good and faithful servant! You have been faithful with a few things; I will put you in charge of many things. Come and share your master's happiness!'"

That's what we all want to hear when we stand before our Lord. The wise Christian steward will follow the cornerstones we're going to outline, but more importantly, she will realize that no amount of money can ever provide ultimate financial security against economic collapse or political upheaval. Following good stewardship principles will result, however, in the confidence of knowing you're doing things as God would have you do them, and consequently as well as they can be done.

Cornerstone One:
A Growing Relationship with God

In John 17:3-4, Jesus said, "Now this is eternal life: that they may know you, the only true God, and Jesus Christ, whom you have sent. I have brought you glory on earth by completing the work you gave me to do." We are here on earth for only a brief time, and while here, we're to bring glory to God by completing the work He gives us. Our ultimate hope is to spend eternity in His presence.

For that reason, the absolute beginning point of successful money management is to have a growing relationship with God. And such a relationship is possible only if we're spending the time to develop it.

One of the first couples Ron ever helped to manage their money was a young physician and his wife. They had become financially successful soon after his medical practice opened and were just completing their dream house. They had planned for and dreamed of this house for years, and now that it was almost complete, they were asking themselves whether it was really a wise use of God's resources.

When they asked Ron whether they should live in that house, he responded with another question: "How much time do you spend in a daily quiet time?" He knew only God could answer their question, so they needed to be asking Him.

The doctor said he just didn't have time for daily devotions. He had to be at the hospital by 6:00 each morning and typically did not get home until 6:00 or 7:00 in the evening. In addition, many times he was on call in the evenings or all night, as well as one or more weekends a month.

He was a godly man, and his wife was a godly woman. They never missed church, loved each other, were doing a good job of raising their children and were more than tithing their income. But he just didn't think he could find the time for daily prayer and Bible study.

"What are you doing at 5:00 in the morning?" Ron asked him.

"Usually I'm asleep," he answered.

"Well, then," Ron said, "my suggestion would be to take the next thirty days and spend ten minutes at 5:00 in the morning in prayer and Scripture meditation, asking God the question you're asking me."

This young doctor was defensive at first, but he began to spend ten minutes a day in prayer and meditation. Over the months that followed, he and Ron had many conversations in which Ron encouraged him to keep seeking the Lord's will in his financial decisions.

A year after that first meeting, his wife told Ron that not only was he spending an *hour* a day developing a relationship with God, but he was also memorizing Scripture, teaching an evangelistic Bible class at the hospital, taking increasing responsibilities at church and so on.

Interestingly, over the years this man has stopped asking Ron how to spend the resources God has given to him. Instead, Ron's role is to help him determine how best to meet his God-given goals. Money has become far less of an issue with him. (By the way, the doctor and his wife did move into their dream house.)

A growing relationship with the Lord will, at a minimum, result in a changed life, as that doctor discovered. Specifically, the following things will happen to your perspective on money.

Perspective on Ownership

First, people who are growing in their relationship with God understand that He is the *source* and *owner* of everything. We read in 1 Timothy 6:6-8, "But god-

> *K*nowing God is the source and owner of all gives us the only valid perspective on money.

liness with contentment is great gain. For we brought nothing into the world, and we can take nothing out of it. But if we have food and clothing, we will be content with that."

It's really true that we brought nothing into this world and that no one has ever taken anything out. You never see a hearse pulling a U-Haul trailer. Knowing

God is the source and owner of all gives us the only valid perspective on money: Money is a *tool* to be used to accomplish His purposes.

We are stewards of God's resources. That means every spending and investing decision should be under His authority and according to His will as best we can discern it. And if the Master chooses to take back whatever is His, that's His right; we have only responsibilities. There's great freedom in being a manager of someone else's property as opposed to being the owner. Financial *bondage* occurs when we take ownership rights to which we have no claim.

Contentment

A growing relationship with the Lord also results in contentment. Hebrews 13:5 says, "Keep your lives free from the love of money and be content with what you have, because God has said, 'Never will I leave you; never will I forsake you.' So we say with confidence, 'The Lord is my helper; I will not be afraid. What can man do to me?'"

We read in Luke 3:14, "Then some soldiers asked him, 'And what should we do?' He replied, 'Don't extort money and don't accuse people falsely—be content with your pay.'" God is the source of our income, and being content with what we earn and learning to live within that are two of the real keys to financial success.

Our desire should be to say with the apostle Paul, "I have learned to be content whatever the circumstances. I know what it is to be in need, and I know what it is to have plenty. I have learned the secret of being content in any and every situation, whether well fed or hungry, whether living in plenty or in want. I can do everything through him who gives me strength" (Phil. 4:11-13).

Proverbs 19:23 sums it up: "The fear of the Lord leads to life: then one rests content, untouched by trouble."

Confidence

A growing relationship with God also results in increasing confidence in His wisdom. "'For who has known the mind of the Lord that he may instruct him?' But we have the mind of Christ" (1 Cor. 2:16). Believing God is giving us His wisdom, which we have by asking Him (see James 1:5), provides the confidence to obey even when it seems foolish from the world's perspective. Knowing God owns it all gives us a confidence to use His resources to accomplish His purposes—to be salt and light in a world that desperately needs both (more about that later in this chapter).

Communication

A growing relationship with the Lord also results in better communication with husbands, parents, children and counselors. When you're content and have confidence in God's wisdom, communication with anyone becomes more effective.

Money as Provision

As we stated earlier, money is never an end in and of itself. Rather, it's a means used to accomplish God's purposes. A common word in the Bible related to money is *provision*. Money is God's provision for the purposes He has set before us. Those purposes include the following:

For God's work
God's work is clearly one of the uses to which His people should put money, just like Nehemiah in the Old Testament: "I also made provision for contributions of wood at designated times, and for the firstfruits" (Neh. 13:31). Under the Lord's direction, Nehemiah made provisions for the rebuilding of Jerusalem's walls. David made sure there were provisions for Solomon to build the temple (see 1 Chron. 22).

For our families
The apostle Paul told us, "If anyone does not provide for his relatives, and especially for his immediate family, he has denied the faith and is worse than an unbeliever" (1 Tim. 5:8). That pretty well says it all.

For future needs
Joseph said in Genesis 45:11, "I will provide for you there, because five years of famine are still to come. Otherwise you and your household and all who belong to you will become destitute." Joseph was providing for his relatives, but he was also providing for the future needs of the entire Egyptian population. Saving and setting aside for the future is not a lack of faith but a wise stewardship decision consistent with biblical teaching.

For the poor

Jesus commanded the money-loving rich young ruler in Mark 10:21, "Sell everything you have and give to the poor." Throughout Scripture, we are told to provide not only for the poor, but also for the hungry, the widow and the orphan.

For other believers

In Acts 11:29, we see the example of the disciples providing for Christian brothers: "The disciples, each according to his ability, decided to provide help for the brothers living in Judea." We can help fellow Christians in many ways, and one of the best is by giving some of the financial resources God has entrusted to us as there is need.

For our employees

We're also commanded in the Bible to provide for those who work for us. "Masters, provide your slaves with what is right and fair, because you know that you also have a Master in heaven" (Col. 4:1). Again, God entrusts us with money to provide for others.

This listing of biblical purposes for money is not meant to be exhaustive. Rather, we offer it to demonstrate that God has a lot to say in His Word about money and how it's to be used.

Money as a Tool, Test and Testimony

As we grow in our relationship with God, we also see more and more how He uses money in our lives as a tool to help us grow spiritually, as a test of our faithfulness and as a testimony to the world. Whenever we experience financial difficulty, we shouldn't ask "Why?" but "What would You have me to learn in this situation?"

Tool

As we previously saw in Philippians 4:11-13, Paul said he had learned to be content whatever the circumstances. He went on to say he had experienced both plenty and want. God uses money as a very effective tool to get our attention.

It isn't always with a *lack* of money, however, that He gets our attention. A successful businessman recently sold a small part of his operation for $5 million. He has invested most of that money in various places, including a portion in the stock market. Now, whenever the stock market drops, he experiences great uncertainty and fear, even though he has wealth far beyond what he can spend in this life. God wants to speak to that man in his financial uncertainty, just as He wants to speak to us in ours.

Test

Jesus said in Luke 16:11-12, "So if you have not been trustworthy in handling worldly wealth, who will trust you with true riches? And if you have not been

God uses money as a very effective tool to get our attention.

trustworthy with someone else's property, who will give you property of your own?" We don't understand completely, but somehow our eternal reward is tied to our faithfulness in handling the money God has entrusted to us. It's sobering to realize we will be held accountable for how we handle the Master's possessions.

Testimony

God also uses money in our lives as a testimony to the rest of the world. Jesus said:

> You are the salt of the earth. But if the salt loses its saltiness, how can it be made salty again? It is no longer good for anything, except to be thrown out and trampled by men. You are the light of the world. A city on a hill cannot be hidden. Neither do people light a lamp and put it under a bowl. Instead they put it on its stand, and it gives light to everyone in the house. In the same way, let your light shine before men, that they may see your good deeds and praise your Father in heaven. (Matt. 5:13-16)

In a world that daily experiences economic uncertainty, one of our greatest Christian testimonies is that money and possessions are not the source of contentment, peace, joy or eternal happiness. We can enjoy all those things, however, because we know the truth that everything good is wrapped up in our Savior, and money and possessions could never substitute for Him.

God Is the Only Source

Growing in God further means we understand that it is He who provides for our needs, not we ourselves. In fact, there is no certain correlation between how hard we work and how much we make. Scripture makes it clear that we're to work diligently, but the income we earn is in God's hands, and He will meet our needs.

"In vain you rise early and stay up late toiling for food to eat—for he grants sleep to those he loves" (Ps. 127:2). A doctor may work three days a week and earn twenty times what a missionary earns, even though the latter works into the evening and on weekends. That would appear to be an inequity. But Paul wrote, "Whatever you do, work at it with all your heart, as working for the Lord, not for men, since you know that you will receive an inheritance from the Lord as a reward. It is the Lord Christ you are serving" (Col. 3:23-24).

Tremendous freedom comes when we accept our responsibility to work heartily and trust God for our needed income, and then live within that God-given income.

Biblical Priority Uses of Income

As growing Christians, we also learn there are priority uses of the income God has entrusted to us. Specifically, we're to do the following.

Give

First, we're commanded to give. "Honor the Lord with your wealth, with the firstfruits of all your crops" (Prov. 3:9). Paul added in 1 Corinthians 16:2, "On the first day of every week, each one of you should set aside a sum of money in keeping with his income, saving it up, so that when I come no collections will have to be made."

The top priority use of our income, then, is to set it aside regularly for the Lord's work. The amount to be set aside is "in keeping with his income" (NIV) or "as God has prospered you" (KJV). We believe the tithe is the beginning point of giving, and the tithe is in obedience to Proverbs 3:9.

Taxes

The second priority use of our income is found in Romans 13:7: "Give everyone what you owe him: if you owe taxes, pay taxes; if revenue, then revenue; if respect, then respect; if honor, then honor." Jesus Himself said, "Give to Caesar what is Caesar's, and to God what is God's" (Matt. 22:21). We have a clear obligation to pay our taxes regardless of how much or how little we like the government.

Repay debt

Third, we are commanded to repay amounts borrowed. "The wicked borrow and do not repay, but the righteous give generously" (Ps. 37:21). It's not a sin to borrow money, but it is a sin not to repay.

Provide for family needs

Fourth, we are commanded to provide for our families' needs. We looked at 1 Timothy 5:8 earlier as one of the reasons God provides an income to us. He not only gives the income, but He also commands us to use a portion of it to take care of our families.

Unfortunately, the Lord doesn't tell us what an appropriate Christian life-style should be. Is it poverty or luxury? If we believe God has placed us in a particular vocation and a certain income goes along with that vocation, and if we follow those four priorities in the use of our money, we'll have a clear idea of what kind

> *G*od can be fully trusted to give us the income we need to obey His commands for the use of His money.

of life-style is appropriate for where God has placed us. We're responsible to use the money according to His commands. The balance that's left after meeting the four priorities is the amount available to be set aside for the future or spent on the life-style we believe God would have for us.

Many Christians, however, have adopted life-style as their top priority, while their giving falls to a fourth or fifth priority. Their reasoning goes something like this: "I would like to give, but by the time I pay my taxes, repay my debts and provide for my family, there's just not enough to tithe, let alone give above the tithe."

God can be fully trusted to give us the income we need to obey His commands for the use of His money. Our challenge is to prioritize the use of that money in line with the Scriptures. If we do, we will no doubt see what the couple wrote to me in the opening letter of this chapter: "We have no more than we did before, but being better stewards has made all the difference." They are now tithing, paying off their debt and buying another home.

We have just scratched the surface of what God has to say about money management. How we handle money reflects on our spiritual maturity and our character as exhibited to the world. That's why the beginning point of successful money management must be a growing relationship with the Lord that results in a study of His Word. That Word helps us to properly interpret our circumstances, which leads to making wise decisions.

CHAPTER THREE

Cornerstones of Success

Part Two

S arah responded to a radio call-in show on which Ron was a guest. She and her husband lived in a small, midwestern town, and she asked where they should invest some excess money. Sarah said they were saving $500 a month. They were putting some money in a company retirement plan and had $10,000 in a savings account—that was the money they wanted to invest. In addition, they had no debt and bought only used cars, thus avoiding the depreciation (loss in value) borne by new-car buyers.

Ron asked Sarah what they were saving for, and she said they were saving for the down payment on a home and building a nest egg for whatever emergencies might come up.

Knowingly or not, Sarah and her husband were almost guaranteeing themselves financial success, because they were following four principles that will work in every situation. Those principles make up the second of our four cornerstones.

Cornerstone Two: Sound Financial Principles

Spend Less Than You Earn

The first principle—spend less than you earn—is so obvious and so funda-mental to success that you would think everyone would know it intuitively. The reality, however, is that we've become such a credit-oriented society that most Americans are spending *more* than they earn. And they don't even know they're falling further and further behind each month, because they've never prepared a basic financial statement or budget.

"Dishonest money dwindles away, but he who gathers money little by little makes it grow" (Prov. 13:11). To illustrate the truth of that verse, consider this:

*I*t's *amazing how few Americans understand that no family, business or government can survive by spending more than it earns.*

If you save $83.33 a month, you will save $1,000 per year. If that $1,000 could be invested to earn 12.5 percent interest, and if you begin at age 25 to save that $83.33 a month, at age 65 you will have put $40,000 into the account. However, the actual value of what you've saved will be $1,000,000 (before taxes). That's called the magic of compounding, and it demonstrates what can happen when you spend a little less than you earn and save the difference over a long time.

The only way to meet long-term goals is to begin saving in this way and con-tinue for some time, just like Sarah and her husband. The larger the goal, the ear-lier the saving needs to be started. It's amazing how few Americans understand that no family, business or government can survive by spending more than it earns.

Avoid the Use of Debt

Credit is so easy to get that almost everyone finds it difficult to avoid the use of debt, even when we know the truth of Proverbs 22:7: "The rich rule over the poor, and the borrower is servant to the lender." Debt always mortgages the future, and it almost guarantees long-term financial bondage. A woman who with her husband makes a good income asked plaintively, "Why do I have to rely on credit cards to make ends meet?" Those words are the modern, financial equivalent of the sound of rattling chains.

Remember, too, that when you borrow, you put the magic of compounding to work *against yourself* and in favor of the lender. You lose the opportunity to earn interest on the dollars you pay in interest on your loan, and instead the bank takes your dollars and earns additional interest for itself.

Ron wrote a book on debt—when to use it, how to use it and how to get out of it. That book is called *The Debt Squeeze,* and we would recommend it if you have any problem with debt.

Maintain Good Liquidity

Consider what it would be like to never be caught short financially: to always have enough money to take advantage of sales; to pay cash for a car when you need one; to be able to pay the unexpected car repair or medical bill; to be able to buy furniture when it's needed; and so on.

Good liquidity means having enough cash readily available to meet your needs (usually in a savings or money market account). It's like being your own banker. It allows you the flexibility to pay the unexpected bill without going into debt or suffering in some other area of need; it also provides the ability to take advantage of opportunities. Wouldn't that be great?

Ron will never forget telling a man one time that he thought he should make a particular investment. The man's response was "I would love to, but I've got all my assets tied up in cash." That's a very conservative but safe position to be in.

In any time of economic difficulty—be it deflation, inflation, a monetary collapse or even a political upheaval—liquidity is preferable to every other type of asset. Liquidity is money in the bank that allows you to avoid economic uncertainty. Maintaining such liquidity *is* possible.

Keep a Long-Term Perspective

The longer-term the perspective, the better the financial decision that can be made today. Part of our problem in American culture is that we've become very short-term in our thinking. We think *long term* means two days. That attitude was summarized perfectly by the woman who asked Ron, "What's the best way to invest my money to yield a quick return?" (There is no best way; large, quick returns require taking large risks.) We're also unwilling to give up today's desires for future benefits—we demand immediate gratification. Our grandparents, on the other hand, understood that delayed gratification is essential to financial success.

When you take a long-term perspective in your decision making, you do have to give up today's desires in many cases. However, your alternatives are greatly expanded. For example, rather than asking yourself, "Should we take this vacation?" ask yourself, "What's the best use of this money over the long term?" It may be that the vacation *is* the best use, but then again, maybe it's not. By taking a longer-term perspective, however, you tend to make better decisions in the short term.

One way to maintain a long-term perspective is to ask yourself two questions. First, are there any alternative uses for this money? Second, how will this decision affect my long-term financial security? We're not saying you don't spend money in the short term—all of us do every day. But we are saying that when you

*C*hristians are really the only people who can have an eternal point of view on the decisions they make today.

spend in the short term, make sure you've considered the long term first.

Without a long-term perspective, no one would ever enter into a relationship with Jesus Christ. The only reason not to eat, drink and be merry to excess, as both Solomon and Paul said, is that our outlook reaches beyond the grave. Christians are really the only people who can have an eternal point of view on the decisions they make today. That's one reason we give. If we had a short-term, temporal perspective, we would never support Christian causes.

Spending less than you earn, maintaining liquidity, avoiding the use of debt and keeping a long-term perspective will work in any economic or political circumstances. The principles can be applied at any age and to any income level.

Can the principles be ignored in the short term without necessarily causing disaster? Yes. But violating them over the long term will have adverse and potentially even tragic consequences.

Cornerstone Three: Basic Financial Skills

As our children have grown older, we've watched them master waterskiing, softball, basketball, tennis, golf, bicycle riding, gymnastics and so on. All those activities have one thing in common: They're sports requiring skills that are developed by repetition.

You don't develop a skill by watching television or reading books but by *doing* it over and over, learning from your mistakes and making progess as you go along. Once a skill has been developed, however, you can use it whenever you need it and will probably never lose it completely, even after years of idleness.

Prior to becoming a Christian, Ron played a lot of golf and got fairly good at it. After he became a Christian, he didn't play for about fifteen years. Just recently he's taken up the game again, however, so he can play with our boys. And he has noticed, somewhat to his amazement, that his game is probably better today than it was fifteen years ago, even though he hasn't played in all that time.

A financial skill is similar. Once it becomes a part of you, it will always be available to you. The essential financial skills that can be mastered by repetitive practice are:

1. Decision making
2. Goal setting
3. Budgeting
4. Communicating
5. Planning

Decision Making

Decision making is a skill we all possess to some degree, because we're all forced to make decisions every day. What we probably don't have, however, is a good skill that has been willfully developed. Most decisions are made intuitively or by gathering the opinions of others who have no more experience or expertise than we do. A good decision may result, but a decision can never be better than the alternatives considered. Unless the decision-making process reveals all the available alternatives, we limit our ability to make good decisions.

A decision is always a choice among alternatives, and that choice is made in order to accomplish our objectives or meet our criteria. For example, the objective might be to buy a car. The criteria might include a price low enough that you can pay cash, a model with a reputation for dependability, four doors, room for five people and a dog and so on.

Good decisions are made by following this process: First, define what decision you're making. Second, list the criteria the decision must satisfy. Third, prioritize those criteria, because some are more important than others. Fourth, determine what alternatives are available to you. Do your best to find them all; someone who has recently made a similar decision might know of options you hadn't considered. Fifth, gather your facts relative to the alternatives—the pros and cons of each. Sixth, choose the alternative that best meets the criteria.

This process is described in detail in our book *Raising Money-Smart Kids.*

Unfortunately, our inflationary economy often forces women to make painful decisions. Our hearts go out to the mother who told us, "With our government working against family and prices increasing, I often feel forced to work and can't be the mom I want to be."

The key to successful decision making is to know what your criteria are so that when you consider the alternatives, you'll know which one best meets those criteria. Intuitive decision making and votes by your friends, while potentially helpful, are extremely risky. In the chapter for young marrieds, we'll look at the decision-making process as it relates to buying a home.

Goal Setting

Goal setting is another skill that can be developed. It has been estimated that less than 3 percent of Americans have written, long-term financial goals. Not coincidentally, less than 5 percent of Americans ever achieve financial independence. If you aim at nothing, you'll hit it every time.

Having long-term financial goals provides motivation, helps focus our efforts and provides rewards as milestones are achieved along the way.

Financial goal setting is nothing more than putting down on paper what specific goals we would like to accomplish. In the long term, there are only six or seven broad, common goals. These include financial independence, paying off all debt, changing your life-style, increasing your giving, starting your own business, paying for children's college education and taking care of family members who need financial help. Each of those goals can be quantified in terms of the dollar amounts needed and the dates by which they need to be accomplished.

The mere act of putting the goals on paper will start you on the road to accomplishing them.

Budgeting

One of the most hated words associated with money management is *budgeting*. It brings up visions of bondage and restraint. The reality, however, is that a budget is nothing more than a series of decisions made ahead of time that reflect a life-style you have adopted.

A second reality is that once effective budgeting is in place, financial *freedom* results, because there's little anxiety when it comes time to make decisions. For

A budget is nothing more than a series of decisions made ahead of time that reflect a life-style you have adopted.

example, you no longer have to wonder whether you should take a vacation. If it's in the budget, you don't have to question spending the money. If it's not in the budget and you don't have extra money for it, your decision is equally clear. Most of us live day to day just reacting to what happens; a good budget lets us exercise some control with a long-term perspective.

Living by a budget is a skill that can be developed. It takes no more than two years to establish the skill—often less, as in the case of the couple whose letter opened chapter 2—and once it's done, the budgeting process requires just a little time each year. It is probably the most-freeing skill that can be developed.

Communicating

Communicating with a spouse, financial counselors, children, salesmen and real estate agents *will* happen. The only question is whether it will be *effective*. Many books have been written on how to communicate. And communication, just like budgeting, is a skill that can be developed. It requires practice and time, but once mastered, it will provide freedom and confidence.

Planning

Financial planning is a skill as well as a process. It can be learned and then used in any financial situation. Because planning is so important to successful money management, we have included it as a separate cornerstone.

Cornerstone Four: Financial Planning

A woman recently wrote Ron a letter in which she quoted numerous Scriptures that speak of God's provision for His people and of how we should trust in Him and not in riches. She said in part, "In light of these Scriptures and many others, should the church be reading (or writing) books which teach us how to handle our money so we can have a higher standard of living, save for retirement and vacations, and employ certain measures of risk to possibly increase our gains?"

She raises the legitimate question of whether it's wrong to plan from a biblical perspective. According to Matthew 6:25-34, shouldn't we just seek first God's kingdom and trust Him to supply all our needs?

Indeed we should trust Him, and that's the main point of Matthew 6. As we stated earlier, God is the source of all we have, and rather than worry, we can depend on Him to meet our needs. But that *doesn't* mean we shouldn't plan. Trust and good planning are not at odds with each other. There are many cases in the Bible where planning was done with beneficial results.

When Joseph planned for the seven years of famine in Egypt by setting aside resources in the seven years of plenty, he was practicing sound financial planning. When Nehemiah rebuilt the walls of Jerusalem, he spent months in prayer, preparation and planning before he even arrived at the city. The result was, of course, that the walls were built in only fifty-two days. David planned to provide the financial resources for his son Solomon to build the temple, and he collected them before his death.

Jesus Himself, in urging people to count the cost of discipleship before committing themselves to His cause, referred to the wisdom of good financial planning: "Suppose one of you wants to build a tower. Will he not first sit down and estimate the cost to see if he has enough money to complete it? For if he lays the foundation and is not able to finish it, everyone who sees it will ridicule him, saying, 'This fellow began to build and was not able to finish'" (Luke 14:28-30). In Proverbs we read, "Plans fail for lack of counsel, but with many advisers they succeed" (Prov. 15:22)—a clearly implied endorsement of good planning.

From these and many other passages we could cite, we believe planning is biblical. It's also extremely wise for the following reasons.

Peace of Mind

Probably the most-rewarding reason for doing financial planning is the peace of mind that comes with knowing where you're headed and how you're going to get there. Many people who fail to plan are like a person who starts on a trip yet has no idea how long the trip will last or where he's going. The likely result is that he gets nowhere. The same thing happens when people manage their finances with no discernable plan. They are paralyzed with indecision and accomplish little.

Basis of Communication

Developing a financial plan also provides a basis for family communication. During the planning process, the family is required to establish and prioritize goals, and everybody knows what they are. Once the family is committed to a plan, the reason for disagreement—which in most cases is uncertainty—has been handled once and for all in a reasonable and rational manner.

Guide for Decision Making

A financial plan serves as a guide for making ongoing decisions. In fact, many decisions are already made. For example, if the plan calls for the establishment of an IRA for a working wife, then $2,000 has been committed for that objective and is not available for any other use, regardless of how attractive an alternative might look. If money has been allocated for home remodeling or college education, the use of those funds has been locked in, and other possible uses don't even need to be considered. In other words, a financial plan brings order rather than confusion.

A financial plan is drawn up through five sequential steps. The end product is several documents and action steps to be taken. Financial planning, however, is really an *ongoing* process. Goals, circumstances, the economy and needs all change, and every change calls for a reexamination of—and possible revisions to—the initial plan. The seasons-of-life approach we're taking in this book outlines many of the dynamics of a financial plan and the decisions that need to be made at different stages of life.

Figure 3.1 is a financial planning diagram; it does three primary things:

1. Outlines the process of financial planning.

2. Summarizes the almost infinite alternatives in the use of money into a manageable few.

3. Integrates the short range with the long range, and clearly demonstrates the trade-offs.

Any spending decision will meet the need or accomplish an objective of one of eleven planning areas, five in the short term and six in the long term. That's the maximum number; most people will not have six long-term objectives. Therefore, you will be dealing with fewer than eleven planning areas. The process of going through the five steps will enable you to accomplish your unique goals or objectives in a prudent, God-honoring way. (Additionally, the *Master Your Money* book goes into much greater depth on the financial planning process.)

Before you can develop a financial plan, however, you need to understand fully your present situation. The next chapter, including the forms at the end, will guide you in doing just that.

Figure 3.1

FINANCIAL PLANNING STEPS

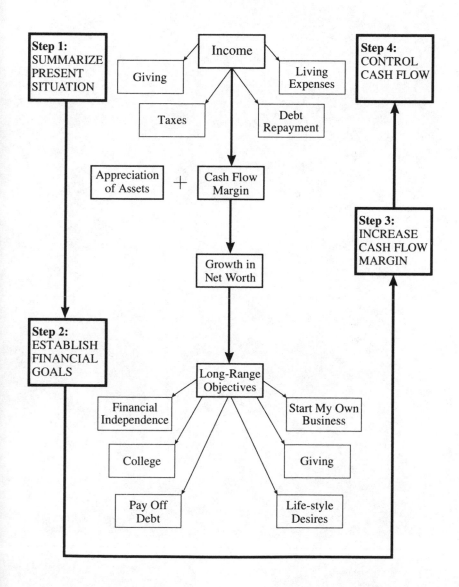

CHAPTER FOUR

Reading the Signs

For recreation, Ron has recently been reading western novels by Louis L'Amour. The following excerpt is from his book *Kiowa Trail* (Bantam, 1964, pp. 116-18): "My mouth felt suddenly dry. Gathering up the reins, I mounted my own horse and started forward, back-tracking the horse.

"The tracks led back up to the prairie, and as it seemed that I might have to ride some distance, I rigged a lead rope for Kate's horse, and started on again.

"There was little daylight remaining. The sun was going down and there would be a brief twilight. And when darkness came I could go no further, but must wait until it was light enough to see tracks again in the grass.

"The horse had trotted here, walked there, stopped to crop grass, then had started on again. It was a once-wild mustang that we had captured and broke to ride ourselves, and he was no stranger to wild country.

"The light faded. I stood up in my stirrups and my eyes searched the ground, but I saw nothing. No one standing, no one walking, no body lying on the grass.

"In the distance, along the horizon, clouds were forming . . . thunder clouds. The air was growing closer, heavier. I moved on, riding parallel to the faint trail. Glancing ahead, I saw the trail across the grass like a faint silver streamer lying along the ground and, touching a spur to my horse, I rode on at a gallop.

"The clouds were piling up rapidly. One of them gleamed suddenly with far-off lightning.

"If the rain came before I found her, the trail would be washed out. In all this vast sweep of prairie there would be no hope of finding Kate Lundy.

"Suddenly, from the southeast, another trail appeared . . . three unshod ponies. That meant Indians.

"Drawing rein, I looked around carefully. With three horses and my weapons, I offered a rare prize for any Indians, and in this country, at this time, they would probably be Kiowas, the most feared of all the tribes of the southern plains.

"The Indians had paused too, studying the lone trail they had come upon. They had ridden along it, one Indian going one way, the others the other. Quickly they had made up their minds—this was a lone, riderless horse.

"The rider was somewhere to the east and south, and that was the way they had gone."

L'Amour's books always seem to have heroes who are "real men" and who end up marrying the heroine. The heroes are also fast with a gun, strong of character, young, handsome and can read a trail like an Indian.

They can tell by looking at hoof prints and following a trail for some distance what kind of horse is up ahead, how heavy the rider is, what the rider's purpose

*B*efore you can make good decisions for your season of life, you must have a good understanding of where you are now.

seems to be, if the rider is having difficulties and so on.

What those heroes do is similar to what we all need to do and what Ron does every day with his clients. That is to learn how to "read" a financial situation from just a few indicators.

When Ron sits down with a couple, he typically has in front of him a statement of net worth, a statement of cash flow, an analysis of insurance coverage and copies of their wills and recent tax returns. From this information he can usually determine their financial strengths and weaknesses, what has gone on in the past, what the future likely holds, problems that need to be solved and decisions that need to be made.

Blank copies of the appropriate forms are located at the end of this chapter. If you'll take the time to fill them out, you'll be able to read them, much as a cowboy would read a trail, to determine where you are financially. This is the necessary first step in the financial planning process, because before you can make good decisions for your season of life, you must have a good understanding of where you are now.

Step 1: Assess Your Current Situation

We assume you've filled out those forms and will refer back to them as you read this next section. What we're going to do now is to help you analyze your own financial situation much as Ron would if you came to him for an initial meeting as a client.

The first thing to look for in surveying your situation is the areas of strength. A large positive net worth is an obvious strength (in other words, assets greater than debts). Be careful, however, to value your assets (what you own) at their *real* value as best you can determine it—not at what you *wish* they were worth. For example, people often overestimate what their cars are worth.

The lower your debt level, the stronger your situation. The *kind* of debt you carry is also significant. Installment debt, credit card debt and consumer debt are never wise to get into. A mortgage, business debt or investment debt, on the other hand, may make some sense in certain situations. For a thorough discussion of the different kinds of debt, please see Ron's book *The Debt Squeeze*.

How much liquidity is reflected on your statement of net worth? As stated earlier, the more liquidity you have, the greater your ability to solve problems and take advantage of opportunities. (On the other hand, even if you have a lot of equity in your house but very little cash, your liquidity is low, and your flexibility is limited.)

Do you have a positive cash flow—that is, do you spend less than you earn? This is essential. Without a positive cash flow, long-term goals *cannot* be met.

Just to pay your bills, you'll either have to sell assets or keep falling deeper into debt. Both of those options bode ill for your future. But a positive cash flow, much like liquidity, gives flexibility as well as peace of mind.

Another important question is whether your cash flow really reflects your priorities. What percentage of your income do you give to the Lord's work? What percentage do you save? Do those two percentages reflect the priorities you would like to have? Is debt taking a high percentage of your cash flow? The national average is approximately 20 percent of cash flow that goes toward the payment of debt (not including a mortgage). That's far greater than it should be.

What percentage of your income is being spent on your life-style (clothes, eating out, recreation, vacations, etc.)? Does that reflect the priority you would like or that God would have for you?

What percentage of your income is going toward taxes? Everyone would like to reduce taxes, but with the low federal income-tax rates we have today, they're seldom a cause of difficulty. (State and local income and property taxes vary widely, of course.)

Is your will up to date or outdated? A will is always important but never urgent until someone dies. If you have no will or your will has not been revised in the last two years, you may have a problem that needs immediate attention.

Is your insurance coverage adequate to provide for death, disability, a long hospital stay or similar catastrophe? We'll be covering this topic in chapters 16-17, but you probably have some feeling already about whether your insurance is adequate.

What kind of investments, if any, do you have? Are they liquid or nonliquid? Are they performing as well as you had expected? How diversified are they? High-yielding, liquid, diversified investments put you in the strongest position. Does your statement of net worth reflect strong investments or weak ones?

An analysis of your financial situation may not reveal any problems to be solved but, rather, decisions to be made: How much to give, to whom and when; how to do a better job of tax planning; where to invest your money; and so on. Whatever the case may be, on a sheet of paper, you need to analyze your financial statements. What are the strengths? What are the weaknesses? *Why* do you have these strengths and weaknesses? What needs to be done differently in the future?

If problems do become apparent as a result of your assessment, they almost certainly resulted from a violation of one of the four cornerstones. So the beginning point in solving the problems is to ask yourself which cornerstone was violated. Was it a scriptural principle? a financial principle? Have you done poorly at exercising the skills required? Have you been operating without a plan?

Some of the common problems revealed in such an analysis include the following:

- More debts than assets (i.e., a negative net worth)
- More expenses than income
- More debt than is possible or prudent
- Inadequate funds to meet real short-term or long-term needs
- An inadequate amount of time to generate needed funds (e.g., for a child's college education)
- A cash flow that does not reflect biblical priorities
- Inadequate insurance coverage
- No proper will or estate plan
- Poor investment results
- Poor communication with your spouse

Such problems and others unique to your situation are almost always solved by going back to the basics—that is, understanding and using the four corner-

*B*efore problems can be solved, they must be accurately identified and accepted as problems to be solved.

stones. But before the problems can be solved, they must be accurately identified and accepted as problems to be solved. In other words, they cannot be swept under the rug. Ignoring debt, for instance, will not make it go away.

Step 2: Set Goals

The second step of the planning process is to set financial goals. A goal is an objective toward which you believe God wants you to move, and it has two characteristics.

First, a goal is defined by a quantitative amount—a specific dollar amount that's needed. Second, a definite time frame is set in which the goal is to be accomplished.

If a goal is not quantified by amount and date, it's more a purpose statement, which is broader than a goal. Goals help us to accomplish purposes. One purpose, for example, would be to become financially independent. A goal to help achieve that end is to set aside $2,000 per year in an IRA for thirty years.

Because they're quantified, you can tell whether you're accomplishing goals. You can't tell, except in retrospect, whether you have accomplished a purpose.

Step 3: Make Decisions

The third step in financial planning is to make the decisions that will move you from where you are to where you want to go—in other words, from step one to step two.

Those decisions are expressed in a short-term cash flow plan—also known as a budget. That plan summarizes your decisions in dollars and cents. It's basically a way of allocating your income among the five short-term alternatives (giving, debt repayment, taxes, life-style desires and accumulation) so you'll be accomplishing your goals in each.

In the immediate future, many of your short-term goals won't really be goals but commitments that must be honored (e.g., ongoing debt repayment). Remember, the most-important thing in making this plan is spending less than you earn. Otherwise, you'll never be able to save, and you'll never reach your long-range goals.

Step 4: Control and Monitor

The fourth step is to develop a monitoring and control system to insure that the cash flow plan written in step three is being accomplished.

The simplest monitoring system is an envelope system. When you receive your income, divide it between five envelopes, one for each of the five short-term planning areas. Back when workers were paid in cash and few people had bank accounts, a couple would actually divide their money into five envelopes. Today, we're more likely to use a page in a family accounting book as an "envelope" to "hold" money that's actually part of the total in a checking account.

Regardless, money is spent out of each envelope according to the plan. And spending stops when the envelope is empty. It's that simple.

The book *Master Your Money* outlines some detailed cash flow monitoring systems. Russ Crosson's book *Money and Marriage* also has an extensive cash flow monitoring chapter.

Step 5: Invest the Excess

If your budget from step three and your monitoring system from step four are working, you should have some money left over at the end of each month, even if it's only a small amount. Step five of the process is to decide how to use that money.

A lot of people erroneously think financial planning *begins* with decisions about investing in things like stocks and bonds. However, if you look back at some of the principles we talked about earlier—avoiding the use of debt, maintaining liquidity and being your own banker—you can see that your excess income shouldn't necessarily be used for long-term investments, especially when you're just starting to get your financial house in order. Instead, it might better be used to avoid debt and build liquidity.

In chapter 17 we'll outline a sequential strategy that shows where your excess should be invested, and we'll also discuss investing in a more-traditional sense (stocks, bonds, gold, real estate, etc.).

Determining where you are and what goals you want to accomplish is more important than deciding where your extra money should be invested. If you're spending less than you earn, avoiding the use of debt and maintaining liquidity—even without an investment plan—you *will* be moving toward financial security and lasting success.

Conclusion

To summarize what we've said so far, financial success begins with making sure you have a growing relationship with the Lord. Then you follow biblical principles of money management, develop the skills that will last a lifetime and follow a planning process that leads to goal setting and goal accomplishment.

In the short term, that process will reveal financial problems and the decisions that need to be made in light of your unique circumstances. This chapter will apply whatever your season of life and wherever you might be financially. It's like a blueprint: If you follow it, you'll build financial peace of mind.

Figure 4.1

GOAL SETTING

The foundation of the financial management process is setting goals. Ted Engstrom, executive vice president of World Vision, states, "Prayerful goal setting is practical faith." According to Bruce Wilkinson, president of Walk Thru the Bible, "A goal is the expression of God's will for you" and is a significant source of motivation and navigation for your life. One way to define success is "the continued achievement of God-given goals."

Goal-Setting Suggestions

1. *Brainstorm*. Without criticism of each other, you and your husband should write down every need, concern and desire you can think of. Take as much time as you like. Empty your heart and mind before God, individually.

2. *Identify goals and purposes*. A goal is measurable so that you can tell when you've reached it. A purpose, on the other hand, is a broader statement of desire. For example:

   PURPOSE: To glorify God in my finances.
   GOAL: To increase my giving to 15% of gross income per year.

3. *Prioritize*. Integrate your lists of goals, and set priorities. All your goals can't be accomplished at once. Because you have limited resources, there's no such thing as an independent financial decision. Goals will be in conflict at times, and you'll have to choose which one to accomplish first.

SPECIFIC FINANCIAL GOALS

What are your most-important goals? (Please list in order of importance.)

1. _____

2. _____

3. _____

4. _____

Check each goal below that's important to you, and then prioritize as follows:

A - absolute must   B - strong desire   C - would like to

Goal	Priority	Quantified How Much	By When

GIVING:

____ Would like to give ____% of gross income a year.

____ Would like to make additional gifts as needs arise.

____ Would like to make gifts of particular properties.

____ Would like to increase giving to ____%.

____ Would like to leave assets to God's work by will. If so, what %?

LIFE-STYLE:

____ Would like to provide a college education for our children (child) funding _____% of the costs.

____ Would like to be able to retire at a chosen life-style.

____ Would like to purchase a larger home.

____ Would like to add on to our house.

____ Would like to purchase a new car(s).

____ Would like to travel to _____.

____ Would like to make a major purchase.

____ Would like to establish a family budget.

ESTATE:

____ Would like to accumulate an estate to pass to heirs.

____ Would like to minimize estate taxes.

____ Would like to provide adequate estate liquidity.

____ Would like to provide adequate assets for a surviving spouse and family.

Goal	Priority	Quantified How Much	By When

INCOME TAX:

___ Would like to reduce amount paid in income taxes.

___ Would like to manage and minimize future income-tax liabilities.

ASSET AND LIABILITY MANAGEMENT:

___ Would like to maximize investment income.

___ Would like to establish an emergency fund.

___ Would like to protect assets against inflation erosion.

___ Would like to reduce debt.

___ Would like to invest in own business.

___ Would like to diversify investment portfolio.

PROTECTION:

___ Would like to protect family lifestyle in the event of death.

___ Would like to protect family lifestyle in the event of disability.

___ Would like to protect against other major catastrophe.

OTHER:

Figure 4.2

NET WORTH

ASSETS

A. Bank Accounts, Notes, Money Market Funds:

Category	Name of Institution	Amount
1. Checking Accounts	_____	_____
2. Checking Accounts	_____	_____
3. Savings Accounts	_____	_____
4. Savings Accounts	_____	_____
5. Money Market Account	_____	_____
6. Money Market Account	_____	_____
7. Notes Receivable	_____	_____
8. Certificates of Deposit	_____	_____
9. _____	_____	_____
10. _____	_____	_____

B. Stocks, Bonds, Mutual Funds (excluding Retirement Assets):

Description	No. of Shares or Bond Face Value	Cost	Market Value
1. _____	_____	_____	_____
2. _____	_____	_____	_____
3. _____	_____	_____	_____
4. _____	_____	_____	_____
5. _____	_____	_____	_____

C. Real Estate, Limited Partnerships and Other Investments:

Location & Description	Cost	Date Purchased	Current Value
1. _____	_____	_____	_____
2. _____	_____	_____	_____
3. _____	_____	_____	_____
4. _____	_____	_____	_____
5. _____	_____	_____	_____
6. _____	_____	_____	_____

D. Retirement Assets:

Type of Fund	Present Amount	Where Invested	Interest Rate (if applicable)
1. IRA (husband)			
2. IRA (husband)			
3. IRA (wife)			
4. IRA (wife)			
5. Keogh			
6. Keogh			
7. Pension			
8. Profit Sharing			
9.			
10.			

E. Personal Property and Other Assets:

Description	Est. Current Value
1. Personal Residence	
2. Autos	
3. Personal Property	
4.	

LIABILITIES

Description	Date of First Payment	Beginning Balance	Current Balance	Interest Rate	Term	Payment Amount
1. Home Mortgage						
2. Auto Loan						
3. Credit Cards						
4.						
5.						
6.						

Other information about assets and liabilities:

_____

_____

_____

_____

Figure 4.3

ANNUAL LIVING-EXPENSE SUMMARY

ITEM DESCRIPTION	MONTHLY	QUARTERLY	ANNUALLY
Housing			
Mortgage/Rent	$_____	$_____	$_____
Insurance			
Maintenance/Repairs			
Home Improvements			
Furnishings			
Property Tax			
Maid			
Other			
Utilities			
Electricity			
Gas			
Water/Sanitation			
Telephone			
Other			
Food			
Groceries/Products			
Other			
Clothing			
Husband			
Wife			
Children			
Other			
Transportation			
Car Payments			
Gas/Oil			
Insurance			
License/Tag/Tax			
Maintenance/Repair			
Other			
Entertainment and Recreation			
Eating Out			
Trips/Vacation			
Baby-sitters			
Memberships			
Books/Film/Tapes			
Entertain/Parties			
Cable TV			
Other			

ITEM DESCRIPTION	MONTHLY	QUARTERLY	ANNUALLY
Medical			
Doctor	$	$	$
Dentist			
Therapist/Other			
Drugs/Medicine			
Medical Ins. Premium			
Other			
Life & Disability Insurance Premiums			
Life - Husband			
Life - Wife			
Life - Children			
Disability			
Other			
Children			
Lessons			
Allowances			
Activities			
Lunches			
Other			
Gifts (Non-deductible)			
Christmas			
Anniversary			
Birthday			
Wedding			
Other			
Miscellaneous			
Beauty/Barber			
Laundry/Dry Clean			
Subscriptions			
Cash/Allowance - H			
Cash/Allowance - W			
Postage/Shipping			
Pets: food/vet/license/etc.			
Other			
Education Expenses			
Private School			
Private School			
College Expenses			
College Expenses			
TOTAL LIVING EXPENSES	$	$	$
Charitable Giving			
Local Church			
Other Organizations			
TOTAL CHARITABLE GIVING	$	$	$

Figure 4.4

LIFE INSURANCE

	Insurance Company	Insured	Owner	Benef.	Cash Value	Face Amount	Annual Premium
1.							
2.							
3.							
4.							
5.							
6.							
7.							

DISABILITY INSURANCE

	Insurance Company	Insured	Monthly Benefit	Benefit Period	Waiting Period	Annual Premium	Premium Paid By
1.							
2.							
3.							
4.							

Figure 4.5

INCOME PROJECTIONS

	Year-to-Date	Year-End	Next Year
Salary	$	$	$
Bonus			
Interest			
Dividends			
Installment Sales			
Notes Receivable			

CHAPTER FIVE

Getting Started: Young Single

God has blessed us with five children, three of whom are young, single women at the time of this writing. One is just entering college, one is about to graduate from college, and the third is now a professional woman. Fortunately, they will not make the same mistakes entering marriage as two other young women we know.

One of those women married a wealthy man several years ago. But while still single, she had accumulated more than $5,000 in credit card debt that she felt she should pay off before she got married. It was painful for her to recognize why she was in debt and then endure the long, slow process of repaying all that money before marriage. She was so affected by the experience that she helped to set up a credit counseling agency working through churches in her area.

Our oldest daughter recently told us the story of the other young woman. She was engaged to be married within a couple of weeks at the time she talked to our daughter. It seems that she and her fiancé had never discussed how each of them handled their finances, and the young man discovered just before the marriage that his bride-to-be had accumulated a fairly large amount of credit card debt. After their marriage, of course, he would be jointly responsible for repaying that debt.

The young man didn't call off the wedding, but he was stunned by the financial obligation he was taking on. He described his experience to a friend who was also to be married in the near future, and that young man immediately went to his fiancée to learn her level of debt before he was willing to set a marriage date.

Our observation of the Christian singles' scene is that it's very entertainment oriented. The pressure to spend money on shows, restaurants, cars, clothes, apartments and so on is incredibly difficult to withstand.

This pressure to spend on short-term desires comes at a time when the first real income is being earned. It's like adding fuel to a fire. The rising income is the fuel. The more fuel you add, the hotter the fire gets. Very quickly, the biggest financial concern can become how to make ends meet.

As if the pressure to spend and spend weren't bad enough, the chances are also good that today's young woman has been poorly trained to handle money and make financial decisions. She gets very little training at church and probably very little in high school or college. Her parents have not always been the best example and probably haven't even thought through how to train a daughter in this area. The flight attendant described in chapter 1 is typical of the way many young women enter adulthood and for the first time must manage money and make financial decisions.

Our objective for our daughters is that when they graduate from college and begin to manage their own income, whether or not they get married, they will accomplish the following:

1. Tithe on their gross (before-tax) income.
2. Have no debt.
3. Have a significant savings account.
4. Manage their monthly expenses by a budget.
5. Know how to use credit cards responsibly.
6. Know how to manage a checking account.

If they enter marriage with those six things working for them, the young men they marry will be lucky indeed. And if they never do marry, they're started down the road to financial success on their own. In fact, we advise them to plan as if they will never get married. That way, if the Lord gives them godly husbands, they will be fortunate young men. But if God does not choose to give them husbands, they will still enjoy financial security and freedom.

You might want to adopt those six goals for yourself. We'll cover each of them in detail in this chapter, as well as some other major financial questions you're

> *P*
> *lan financially as if you'll never get married. That way, if the Lord gives you a godly husband, he will be a fortunate young man.*

likely to face: life insurance, buying a house versus renting, buying cars, establishing medical insurance coverage and planning and managing for income taxes.

Bear in mind also that a young, single woman has minimal long-range planning needs. College education for children is not a concern, life-style desires can be funded by current income, owning a business is probably not yet a long-term goal, and even retirement is so far down the road that it's not an overriding goal. Therefore, most of the financial planning decisions will be short range in nature.

Establish the Tithe Habit

Two of our daughters are sponsoring children through relief organizations every month. Both of them made the decision to do this giving above and beyond their tithe without consulting anyone else in the family. They made their decisions out of a conviction that it was what God would have them do.

There may be no more controversial issue in the Christian life—and probably no greater issue of disobedience—than tithing and giving. How much to give, when and to whom are some of the most-difficult questions for any Christian to answer, let alone young singles.

According to an article in *Moody Monthly* written by Sylvia and John Ronsvalle, the current per capita giving in all North American evangelical churches is about 2.5 percent. According to the Internal Revenue Service, the average charitable giving of all Americans is only 1.7 percent of adjusted gross income.

Obviously, on the average, Americans give nowhere near a tithe amount of 10 percent—not even evangelical Christians. In fact, evangelical Christians give only slightly more than all other Americans.

In 1 Corinthians 16:2, Paul said, "On the first day of every week, each one of you should set aside a sum of money in keeping with his income, saving it up, so that when I come no collections will have to be made." Additionally, Proverbs 3:9-10 says, "Honor the Lord with your wealth, with the firstfruits of all of your crops; then your barns will be filled to overflowing, and your vats will brim over with new wine."

The conclusions are that the obedient Christian should:

1. Give regularly.
2. Give proportionately as God has prospered.
3. Give off the gross receipts of income.

The beginning point of giving is at least 10 percent—that is, the tithe. By giving the tithe, we recognize that God owns it all. Our reading of the Scriptures is that true giving doesn't even begin until one has at least recognized God's ownership by tithing.

We understand, of course, that we are now under grace rather than the Law, and therefore we may not be subject to the same strict interpretations of the Old Testament Scriptures as were the Jews to whom the Law was addressed. However, we frankly don't understand why Christians who realize they have been given eternal life would want to give less than a tenth of their income to the Lord's work.

We're not saying that tithing is a Christian law. Nor do we give it to receive a blessing. It is, however, an amount that expresses clear recognition of God's ownership.

Giving should also be done regularly so that it becomes habitual. One of the reasons we feel so strongly about giving is that it establishes the priorities in using the rest of our income. When we give as a first priority, we're saying that

God is the source of that income and is the first priority in every area of our lives. There is no more-tangible evidence of God's preeminence in our lives than giving Him our tithes.

We realize it's difficult for a young, single woman to tithe regularly. For the first time in her life, she's earning good money, and giving away a significant part

Tithing is the first real financial test of faith that any of us experience.

of it conflicts with her desire to accomplish some short-term goals. She wants to buy furniture and clothes, travel, perhaps even purchase her first car. To tithe her income limits her ability to do those things.

Therefore, the only way a young woman will tithe her income is if she does it as an act of faith, recognizing that God owns it all and wanting to obey His Word. Tithing is the first real financial test of faith that any of us experience. We know intuitively that giving away money with no tangible, immediate benefit is costly. Unless we trust that God and His Word are true and trustworthy, we'll never take that step of faith.

The Eighth Wonder of the World

If we told you we could show you how to turn a $20,000 investment into something worth between $500,000 and $1 million with minimal risk, we're sure you would be interested. And in fact, it *is* possible to accumulate large sums of money just by using the eighth wonder of the world, the magic of compounding.

Three variables affect how much you earn from an investment—how much compounding works to your advantage. They are the length of time available, the amount invested and the interest rate earned. Two of those, the time and the amount, you control; the third you don't.

To demonstrate the interaction of those three elements, we'll use the example of investing in an individual retirement account (IRA). We use that example for two reasons. First, an IRA or other tax-deferred retirement account is a good thing for even a young single to have. It allows you to build savings for long-range goals (like retirement) without paying taxes on the earnings from year to year (you only pay taxes when you withdraw the money later in life). Second, the IRA's tax-deferred status lets us look at how compounding works without the complication of tax considerations.

Suppose that at age twenty you began to invest $2,000 per year in an IRA earning 8 percent per year, and you did that for ten years and then never added another penny to the account. At age sixty-five, you would have accumulated $499,660. That is almost $480,000 in interest earned on a $20,000 investment.

If you wait until age twenty-seven to begin contributing to an IRA, however, you would have to contribute $2,000 per year until age fifty-nine—for a total of thirty-three years—to accumulate a comparable amount of money by age sixty-five. If you contributed from age twenty-seven all the way to age sixty-five, for a total of $78,000, you would have only slightly more than the first illustration.

The first chart (fig. 5.1) compares the two scenarios. Some of you will be married before age thirty, raising a family and not producing an income, and in that case you won't be able to contribute to an IRA. Therefore, you should take advantage of the opportunity to build an IRA while you're still single.

The second chart (fig. 5.2) shows what would happen if your IRA earns 10 percent per year rather than 8 percent—just 2 percent more. The $20,000 invested from ages twenty to twenty-nine will grow to more than twice as much by age sixty-five: $1,083,871.

Figure 5.1

COMPARISON OF IRA FUND GROWTH

Beginning at age 20 vs. age 27 assuming 8% investment growth

Age	Person who begins at age 20			Person who begins at age 27			Difference
	Annual Contribution	Cumulative Contributions	End-of-year Balance	Annual Contribution	Cumulative Contributions	End-of-year Balance	
20	2,000	2,000	2,160				2,160
21	2,000	4,000	4,493				4,493
22	2,000	6,000	7,012				7,012
23	2,000	8,000	9,733				9,733
24	2,000	10,000	12,672				12,672
25	2,000	12,000	15,846				15,846
26	2,000	14,000	19,273				19,273
27	2,000	16,000	22,975	2,000	2,000	2,160	20,815
28	2,000	18,000	26,973	2,000	4,000	4,493	22,480
29	2,000	20,000	31,291	2,000	6,000	7,012	24,279
30		20,000	33,794	2,000	8,000	9,733	24,061
31		20,000	36,498	2,000	10,000	12,672	23,826
32		20,000	39,418	2,000	12,000	15,846	23,572
33		20,000	42,571	2,000	14,000	19,273	23,298
34		20,000	45,977	2,000	16,000	22,975	23,002
35		20,000	49,655	2,000	18,000	26,973	22,682
36		20,000	53,627	2,000	20,000	31,291	22,336
37		20,000	57,917	2,000	22,000	35,954	21,963
38		20,000	62,551	2,000	24,000	40,991	21,560
39		20,000	67,555	2,000	26,000	46,430	21,125
40		20,000	72,959	2,000	28,000	52,304	20,655
41		20,000	78,796	2,000	30,000	58,649	20,147
42		20,000	85,100	2,000	32,000	65,500	19,599
43		20,000	91,908	2,000	34,000	72,900	19,007
44		20,000	99,260	2,000	36,000	80,893	18,368
45		20,000	107,201	2,000	38,000	89,524	17,677
46		20,000	115,777	2,000	40,000	98,846	16,931
47		20,000	125,039	2,000	42,000	108,914	16,126
48		20,000	135,042	2,000	44,000	119,787	15,256
49		20,000	145,846	2,000	46,000	131,530	14,316
50		20,000	157,514	2,000	48,000	144,212	13,302
51		20,000	170,115	2,000	50,000	157,909	12,206
52		20,000	183,724	2,000	52,000	172,702	11,022
53		20,000	198,422	2,000	54,000	188,678	9,744
54		20,000	214,295	2,000	56,000	205,932	8,364
55		20,000	231,439	2,000	58,000	224,566	6,873
56		20,000	249,954	2,000	60,000	244,692	5,262
57		20,000	269,951	2,000	62,000	266,427	3,523
58		20,000	291,547	2,000	64,000	289,901	1,645
59		20,000	314,870	2,000	66,000	315,253	(383)
60		20,000	340,060	2,000	68,000	342,634	(2,574)
61		20,000	367,265	2,000	70,000	372,204	(4,940)
62		20,000	396,646	2,000	72,000	404,141	(7,495)
63		20,000	428,378	2,000	74,000	438,632	(10,254)
64		20,000	462,648	2,000	76,000	475,882	(13,235)
65		20,000	499,660	2,000	78,000	516,113	(16,453)

Figure 5.2
COMPARISON OF IRA FUND GROWTH
Beginning at age 20 vs. age 27 assuming 10% investment growth

	Person who begins at age 20			Person who begins at age 27			
Age	Annual Contribution	Cumulative Contributions	End-of-year Balance	Annual Contribution	Cumulative Contributions	End-of-year Balance	Difference
20	2,000	2,000	2,200				2,200
21	2,000	4,000	4,620				4,620
22	2,000	6,000	7,282				7,282
23	2,000	8,000	10,210				10,210
24	2,000	10,000	13,431				13,431
25	2,000	12,000	16,974				16,974
26	2,000	14,000	20,872				20,872
27	2,000	16,000	25,159	2,000	2,000	2,200	22,959
28	2,000	18,000	29,875	2,000	4,000	4,620	25,255
29	2,000	20,000	35,062	2,000	6,000	7,282	27,780
30		20,000	38,569	2,000	8,000	10,210	28,358
31		20,000	42,425	2,000	10,000	13,431	28,994
32		20,000	46,668	2,000	12,000	16,974	29,694
33		20,000	51,335	2,000	14,000	20,872	30,463
34		20,000	56,468	2,000	16,000	25,159	31,309
35		20,000	62,115	2,000	18,000	29,875	32,240
36		20,000	68,327	2,000	20,000	35,062	33,264
37		20,000	75,159	2,000	22,000	40,769	34,391
38		20,000	82,675	2,000	24,000	47,045	35,630
39		20,000	90,943	2,000	26,000	53,950	36,993
40		20,000	100,037	2,000	28,000	61,545	38,492
41		20,000	110,041	2,000	30,000	69,899	40,141
42		20,000	121,045	2,000	32,000	79,089	41,955
43		20,000	133,149	2,000	34,000	89,198	43,951
44		20,000	146,464	2,000	36,000	100,318	46,146
45		20,000	161,110	2,000	38,000	112,550	48,560
46		20,000	177,222	2,000	40,000	126,005	51,217
47		20,000	194,944	2,000	42,000	140,805	54,138
48		20,000	214,438	2,000	44,000	157,086	57,352
49		20,000	235,882	2,000	46,000	174,995	60,887
50		20,000	259,470	2,000	48,000	194,694	64,776
51		20,000	285,417	2,000	50,000	216,364	69,054
52		20,000	313,959	2,000	52,000	240,200	73,759
53		20,000	345,355	2,000	54,000	266,420	78,935
54		20,000	379,890	2,000	56,000	295,262	84,628
55		20,000	417,879	2,000	58,000	326,988	90,891
56		20,000	459,667	2,000	60,000	361,887	97,780
57		20,000	505,634	2,000	62,000	400,276	105,358
58		20,000	556,197	2,000	64,000	442,503	113,694
59		20,000	611,817	2,000	66,000	488,953	122,863
60		20,000	672,998	2,000	68,000	540,049	132,950
61		20,000	740,298	2,000	70,000	596,254	144,045
62		20,000	814,328	2,000	72,000	658,079	156,249
63		20,000	895,761	2,000	74,000	726,087	169,674
64		20,000	985,337	2,000	76,000	800,896	184,441
65		20,000	1,083,871	2,000	78,000	883,185	200,686

Obviously, the sooner you start, the better off you'll be. Where you invest isn't nearly as important as *beginning* an investment program. Most banks, insurance companies, brokerages and mutual funds offer IRAs. We suggest you begin by establishing an IRA someplace you're familiar with, and then, over time, educate yourself about where else it's possible to invest IRA money. You can move from one investment vehicle to another without paying taxes or penalties, so you can always switch later to something paying a higher rate of interest if you so choose. Remember, however, that you can't invest anywhere until you're spending less than you earn.

Another way to see the impact of compounding is to compare making an IRA contribution at the earliest possible time (Jan. 1) to making it at the latest possible time (April 15 of the following year, or fifteen and a half months later). Contributions can be made at any time during that period.

If you invest $2,000 a year for thirty years and earn 10 percent interest, investing on January 1 will result in an accumulation of $397,362. Waiting until April 15 of the following year will yield an accumulation that's $54,637 less, even though the time period, the amount invested and the interest rate are all the same. The loss in what could be earned may represent several years of retirement living expenses.

The best alternative, then, is to put $2,000 in an IRA as early in the year as possible. The next-best alternative is to fund an IRA through monthly deposits.

Sequential Investing

The sequential investment plan answers many questions about where to invest money, paying off debt versus savings, how much liquidity is needed and so on. See chapter 17 for a full discussion of the plan and figure 17.1 for a graphic summary.

Step one of any investment program is to eliminate all high-interest debt. That would include credit card debt, car loans and any other installment debt. Paying off such debt is absolutely the best investment you can make, because it's the equivalent of investing with a return of 12 to 21 percent. Not even the most successful investors can achieve consistent, guaranteed, 12 to 21 percent after-tax rates of return. The reason these are after-tax rates of return is that all such personal interest is basically nondeductible now, so even the interest is paid with after-tax dollars.

The question often comes up, "Should I take money out of savings to pay off that debt?" The answer is generally yes, because as soon as you stop *paying* interest, you can start *earning* it. However, don't leave yourself without money to cover emergencies (usually one to six months of living expenses). Pay off debt only with savings in excess of your emergency fund.

The second investment step is to put one month's living expenses in your checking account. That way, at the beginning of the month you have the month's living expenses covered, and you never run out of income before you run out of month.

The third step is to put three to six months' living expenses in a money market account. This is your emergency fund; it can be used for major purchases such as furniture, unexpected needs such as car repairs and significant opportunities that come along, such as the vacation you don't want to miss. You are effectively becoming your own banker when you reach this step.

Step four is to put money aside every month toward major purchases such as a car or a home down payment. You do this *after* you've taken steps one, two and three. This money should also be invested in a money market fund.

Incidentally, less than 20 percent of all Americans ever achieve step one of this sequential investment strategy. The percentage of young, single women who reach it is most likely even smaller. Obviously, as you go up the steps, the percentage of those who achieve each of them becomes smaller. Perhaps only 10 percent of young, single women ever reach step two, and probably less than 1 percent reach step three.

These observations are not meant to discourage you but rather to encourage you. Following the sequential investment strategy is really very simple, especially if you begin now, when your responsibilities are limited. The problem most people have with the strategy (besides ignorance) is not with the method but with the discipline of spending less than they earn so they have something to invest in the first place. If you can develop that discipline now, you'll be miles ahead of most people and well on your way to true peace of mind.

Step five is where you begin to invest to meet long-term goals. As a young single, you probably won't try to do this (except through an IRA) until you approach about age thirty. But if you reach this stage, read chapter 17 for the basics of investing.

Step six is what we traditionally call investing, and few people ever reach it. When and if you do, you'll need expert help to make good choices. (Chap. 14 tells how to find such help.)

The Pitfalls of Debt

Debt is such a major topic that Ron wrote an entire book about it (*The Debt Squeeze,* Focus on the Family, 1989). The book was needed because more than 80 percent of Americans owe more than they own. In addition, approximately 20 percent of all income goes toward the payment of consumer and credit card debt. That doesn't include mortgage payments. Access to credit has become so easy that it's almost impossible to avoid the trap of debt. If you, just starting out financially, can stay out of that trap, you'll again be miles ahead of most people, both now and throughout your life.

Accordingly, we offer three pieces of advice:

1. Avoid credit card, consumer and installment debt at all costs—at the cost of buying a used car as opposed to a new one; at the cost of having old furniture rather than new.

2. Pay off all credit card balances entirely at the end of each month. Never, ever incur a credit card interest charge. Paying the interest on credit card debt is the most-expensive way to buy anything. It can add 20 percent per year to the cost of whatever you buy.

3. Always, always pay cash for cars (more on that a little later in this chapter).

If you're already in debt, waste no time beginning a repayment plan to get out of it. There's probably no easier time to work your way out of debt than when you're a young single. If you need to make a temporary reduction in your lifestyle, it will probably require only a minimal sacrifice, and no one else is affected, either.

We also recommend that you hold yourself accountable to someone while you're trying to get out of debt so that you don't waver under the pressures your peer group will bring against you because you're attempting to do something different. Very few young, single women forgo the use of debt, yet they're mortgaging their future and potentially their families' future.

How should you respond to unsolicited credit card offers? Getting an offer in the mail doesn't make you credit worthy. It just means you're on a mailing list. To lenders, credit worthiness means you use credit to buy things you can't afford and are willing to pay interest rates that make no sense to anyone except the lender. It's a statistical fact that putting a credit card in a person's hand will cause her (or him) to spend up to 34 percent more than if she uses cash.

Therefore, if you receive an unsolicited credit card offer, toss it into the trash can immediately. If they send you the actual card, cut it up and mail it back or throw it away.

Budget: Another Name for Freedom

When the word *budget* is mentioned, almost invariably people think about constraints, inflexibility, rigidity and guilt. In reality, however, living with a budget is the same thing as taking a trip with a preplanned route—and that route leads to true freedom.

A budget is just a short-term spending plan; preparing one simply means you decide ahead of time how you're going to spend your income. The mere exercise of writing a budget will give you greater confidence in your financial situation than just about anything else you could do. And the absolute best time to start the budgeting process is right now, when you have few categories, total control over your income and no one else for whom you're responsible.

When you prepare a budget, priorities are set. The process helps you to avoid debt and spot potential problems. The charts at the end of chapter 4 can be used to set up a first budget. (Obviously, they'll need to be modified to fit your unique situation.)

You'll notice there are three columns for monthly and periodic expenses and the total annual amount. That's because some expenses are paid every month, whereas others occur infrequently during the year but in a larger lump sum—for example, vacation, insurance premiums, car repairs and so forth.

The larger, periodic amounts are what tend to break a budget, because they're often overlooked. One woman whose experience is typical told us, "Even though we know how to fill out a budget, we have difficulty living it daily. Surprise happenings come often that blow everything off the budget." We all sympathize and nod our heads in agreement, but we should also realize that such "surprises" are a part of life and budget accordingly.

Elizabeth, a young single, told us how she controls her budget once it's set. She divides all her expenses into five categories and keeps one envelope for each. Her categories are:

- overhead: rent and tithe
- loan payments: student loan, parents' loan
- food and fun: groceries and entertainment
- credit card charges: gasoline and travel
- utilities: phone, electricity and so on

Each month, Elizabeth puts the amount of cash she needs into these envelopes and carries them with her in her purse. If she writes a check or uses a credit card, she records the check on the outside of the envelope or puts the credit card receipt in the envelope. At the end of the month, she knows how much she has spent in each category and can compare the amount to what she had budgeted. For those envelopes that literally have cash in them, she stops spending when the envelope is empty. (That, incidentally, is the key to controlling a budget.)

As Elizabeth has progressed in her budget control system, she says she learned it could not be cumbersome. She began with many envelopes and eliminated most of them as time went on. She uses credit cards only for travel and major purchases, and the balances are always paid off at the end of the month.

A couple of budgeting concepts are important to understand. First, a budget is not set in stone for all time. You can change it when you get new information. A budget is not the law; it's a guideline to be followed. When it becomes a law, it's a taskmaster worthy of all the negative thoughts people usually have about budgets. But when it's a guideline to be followed and it can be changed as needed, a budget is a friend.

Second, remember that when you get a raise, not all of that money is available to be spent. Your tithe should be increased in line with your higher gross income. Your taxes will go up. And some of the money should be put in savings as you follow the sequential investment plan. Whatever is left is the amount available to be spent on your life-style.

A budget brings freedom and decreases confusion, fear and frustration. Elizabeth says that prior to instituting her simple budgeting system, she lived in constant fear of running out of money. She never had a short-range spending plan, so she was constantly frustrated and uncertain when it came to making decisions. Not until she learned how to budget did she find real financial freedom. She had no more income, but planning how that money was to be spent gave her a tremendous sense of security and peace of mind.

We encourage you to begin budgeting if you're not already doing so. Like Elizabeth, you will experience a greater level of financial freedom. To get the full benefit of budgeting, of course, you'll always need to balance your checkbook at the end of the month. If you don't know how to do that, either a banker or a friend can show you. Don't be embarrassed to ask for help; we all have to learn from others.

Taxes

Everyone would like to pay less in taxes. For some people, there's also a fairness issue. As one woman told us, "I can't feel good about paying my taxes honestly when corporations pay so little and get richer and richer." Whether her perception is accurate or not, the feelings are real and quite common.

Before you put too much effort into thinking about how to reduce your taxes, however, realize there are really only two ways: you must either reduce your income or increase your expenses. Both are costly and ill advised.

Therefore, we have two recommendations regarding taxes. First, *never increase your expenses just to get a tax deduction.* That's always more costly than the benefits received. For example, if you increase your deductible interest expenses by $1,000 and you're in the 25 percent tax bracket, your taxes go down only $250. In other words, you have paid $750 out of your pocket to reduce your taxes $250. That never makes good sense.

Second, never get a tax refund; a refund is a sign of poor planning. That may sound strange at first, as many people look forward to receiving a big refund each year. However, *you're never obligated to pay any more through withholding or tax estimates than what you will actually owe.* When you get a refund, it means that instead of having that money to use during the year—and remember it's *your* money—you've been giving the government an interest-free loan, and they didn't even have to ask your permission!

If you file the IRS's short form tax return (form 1040A), you can know with certainty ahead of time what your taxes are going to be and set your withholdings accordingly by going to your employer and changing your form W-4. If you file the long form (1040), you can estimate your tax liability by taking last year's return and filling in the current year's numbers. Then, again, go to your employer, and set your withholdings accordingly on your form W-4.

Insurance

As a young single, your primary insurance needs are for your health and your car. You might want to buy life insurance to cover any debts you have, as well as burial expenses. Otherwise, you would buy life insurance only if you wanted to leave money to family, friends or charity.

Life insurance is not usually a good investment vehicle, so it shouldn't be used that way. You don't really need to understand all the intricacies of life insurance at this stage of your life, but if you'd like additional information, chapter 15 describes how to plan a life insurance program at the appropriate time.

Buying Cars

The two most significant buying decisions you'll face at this stage of life are what kind of car to buy and how, and whether or not to buy a home. Let's look first at buying a car.

The first rule in purchasing a car is that you should always pay cash after saving for it ahead of time.

Ron made that recommendation to a singles' Sunday school class just recently, and a young woman challenged him as he has never been challenged in any group before. She said she didn't mean to imply he was a male chauvinist but that he could in no way understand a young, single woman if he would make that suggestion. She was irate at the idea that she should drive an older car. Didn't he comprehend her need to have a new and "safe" car?

Ron didn't want to embarrass her in front of the class by pointing out the fallacy of her thinking. However, if you can't afford to save for a car, you can't afford to borrow for it, either. In other words, looking at the other side of the same coin, if you can afford to make monthly payments, you can afford to make monthly payments *ahead of time*—that is, *save* for a car. It may mean you drive an older car or your current car for a longer time before you purchase the new car, but it can be done.

Research shows that absolutely the cheapest car you will ever drive is the car you presently own. The cost of replacement and the incidental costs of a new car far outweigh the repair and maintenance costs of an older car. It's never advantageous from a purely economic standpoint to replace your car.

For obvious reasons, we would never recommend you drive an unsafe car. An older or used car doesn't have to be mechanically unreliable or unsafe, however. Many people trade or sell cars after just two or three years of ownership, so lots of safe cars are available at reduced prices for those willing to drive them.

The men in your singles' department, or perhaps your father or brother, can help you evaluate mechanically any car you're thinking of buying. A used car can also be taken to a service station or mechanic to be tested before you close the deal.

In preparation for buying a car, put a car payment in your monthly budget. Don't actually go into debt to buy a car, but put the equivalent of a car payment into a savings account each month so that when it comes time to buy a car, or to

*I*f you can't afford to save for a car, you can't afford to borrow for it, either.

replace the one you have now, the cash will be available. Always, always save ahead of time to buy a car. You should always have a car payment, but that payment should go to yourself.

If you don't follow this advice—if you take out a loan to buy a car like most people—you'll be on the wrong side of the magic of compounding. Instead of earning interest on your savings, the bank will be earning interest on your payments. Lenders know this, which is why they're so ready to loan you money.

When Cynthia, our oldest daughter, graduated from college, one of the things Ron wanted to teach her was how to bargain for a car. The beginning point is to know exactly what you want to buy. That way, your bargaining is over price and not features. Anyone who's selling a car will want to convince you of the value of the features. But if you've already decided on the features you want, all you're talking about is the cost to buy those features, and you can compare apples to apples.

Ron asked Cynthia to visit several dealerships to determine what features she wanted without even talking about price. She made those visits on her own so that she could learn how to deal with the salesmen who wanted to sell her something immediately.

The second step was for the two of them to visit the dealerships together and determine what their initial offers would be. (Ron went along because Cynthia felt more comfortable that way. You can also take a male friend or relative with you if you like, though it's certainly not essential to the bargaining process.)

The third step was to begin bargaining, and this, frankly, is very difficult for most people. Ron had Cynthia talk to each salesman and ask him to give her his best price. She then went from salesman to salesman, telling them what was the best price she had been quoted. In every case they lowered the price until she eventually got to a point where no one would lower his price further.

The amount she ultimately paid was about 15 percent below the sticker price. Incidentally, it made no difference to the dealer whether she paid cash or financed the car. He was incredulous that she was going to pay cash because it was so unusual, but in terms of the price it made no difference.

Bargaining takes courage, but it results in the lowest price possible for a car. As long as you're willing to walk away from the purchase, the price will continue to come down. The key is to have more than one alternative that will meet your needs; that puts you in a much better bargaining position.

The process itself is not difficult, and we encourage you to never pay the asking price, even if you're buying a used car. Determine what you want, compare prices between dealers and relative to the information in a guidebook like the bankers' blue book of used-car values, and then play each salesman or seller against the others until you have the lowest price possible.

Buy or Rent

"For a college graduate who is single and just beginning to live independently, which is the best option: to rent an apartment or invest in some sort of real estate?" The young woman who asked us that question was voicing a choice facing every young single. In the next chapter for young marrieds, we're going to cover that decision in detail, but a couple of things are worth considering at the young single stage of life.

First, a home you buy becomes a nonliquid asset, and it certainly limits your financial flexibility. In other words, it ties up a lot of your money, and it can't be sold quickly or easily should the need arise (unless you're willing to sell at well below its true value). Ownership also requires a lot of money for upkeep, repairs and property taxes. Additionally, as recent years have shown, home ownership isn't even the guaranteed-good inflation hedge many thought it would always be, as home prices fell all over the country.

For some young, single women, the physical and time demands of mowing the grass, fixing leaky roofs, replacing worn-out furnace filters, painting, redecorating and so on make even the economic benefits of home ownership, if there are any, not enough to make them buy. There's a real cost to home ownership in terms of time, commitment and loss of flexibility.

That's not to say home ownership is wrong, of course. But given the flexibility that comes with living in an apartment, it seems the better alternative for most young singles. We rarely counsel anyone to buy a home for investment purposes. Homes should be purchased primarily because that's the life-style you want and you're willing to pay for it.

Conclusion

A young, single woman lives with a tremendous amount of uncertainty: she may or may not get married and have a family. And depending on her desire to do so, she can be paralyzed with financial indecision. Our recommendation is that you assume you're not going to get married and live as if you're going to have to support yourself for the rest of your life. Then, if you do get married, you'll be bringing a strong financial base into the marriage instead of credit card debt, car payments and so on.

As a young person, time is your ally. Even though you may have made some mistakes, you have much time to recover. This chapter, we hope, has given you some guidance in the decisions you should make. However, there will no doubt be other issues that come up for which you'll need counsel and assistance. That's where the body of Christ comes in, and you should feel the freedom to ask for the help of older members. The one sure way of getting wisdom is to learn from making mistakes, and many of those who are older have already made the mistakes about which we forewarn you in this chapter.

One young woman, when asked about her major financial questions, answered, "When do I begin playing like an adult?" She was almost thirty years old, and what she meant was, "Do I keep managing my money as I see my young friends doing it, or do I now settle down and begin managing it responsibly?"

We suggest you begin acting like an adult immediately. There's no age at which you automatically pass into adulthood. Rather, adulthood is a reflection of maturity, and you should begin acting maturely now. You'll be glad you did for the rest of your life.

CHAPTER SIX

Bridging the Coping Gap: Young Married

Several years ago, we began to teach a young marrieds' Sunday school class at our church. This was a group of sharp couples who had been married any time from a few weeks to five years. The first Sunday we taught, we went around the room and asked each person what had been the biggest adjustment in marriage. Probably the most-humorous answer came from the young man who said that after growing up in a family of boys, he'd had to learn to put down the toilet seat!

There were also many serious comments, however, and as we summed it up later, the biggest adjustment seemed to come in the area of financial expectations. Specifically, they entered marriage thinking they could *start* where their parents had left off: a house full of furniture, two cars, resort vacations, all the clothes they needed and all the toys they wanted—VCRs, lawn equipment, boats and so on. Never mind that their parents had worked years and years to accumulate such things.

What they described is called a "coping gap." That's the difference between expectations and reality. Their expectation was to start where their parents left off, but the reality was that they couldn't afford such a life-style. They had to learn to adjust to the resulting coping gap.

Each young couple must also face the coping gap that grows out of the differences between their individual expectations. When the two of us got married, we didn't envision there would ever be any differences in our goals, desires or needs. A few hours into our honeymoon, however, we realized we *did* have differences. And even though those differences have remained small over time in our case, small differences can grow in significance.

When two people get married, they bring together two different sets of priorities, and ultimately all financial decisions are based on priorities. Unless a young husband and wife find a way to agree on priorities, they will experience

Unless a young husband and wife find a way to agree on priorities, they will experience financial problems throughout their married life.

financial problems throughout their married life. As a matter of fact, more than 50 percent of the divorces in America are attributed to financial problems. The reality, however, is that there are *no* financial problems, but there *are* major disagreements about priorities.

Marriage also brings together two different training systems. You may have a spender marrying a saver. You may have a husband coming from a female-controlled family and a wife coming from a male-controlled family, or vice versa. And very likely, you'll have two people who have never been trained in money management.

Two financial situations merge in marriage as well. Two sets of income, savings, debt, assets and investments now become joined. If one partner has a poor credit history and rating, the other spouse must accept and deal with that. A key question will have to be resolved: "Who controls the checkbook; who controls the income?"

According to the nationwide survey commissioned for this book, the biggest fear of young, married women is not being able to make ends meet. There's good reason for that fear. In an article in *Atlanta Weekly Magazine* titled "Down and Out in the Middle Class," business writer David Sylvester described a frustrating dilemma most young marrieds face these days: More than two-thirds of such couples rely on two wage earners already, yet their ability to reach their goals is declining.

Sylvester quoted Frank Levy, a professor of public policy at the University of Maryland, as saying time is running out for those couples: "There is no third earner in reserve to keep consumption growing. The birth rate stopped falling in the late 1970s, and families cannot expect continued reductions in mouths to feed. The rest of the world will not lend us increasing amounts forever."

According to Sylvester, "His [Levy's] conclusion: 'The young middle class, principally the baby boomers, has experienced a dramatic decline in its ability to pursue the conventional American dream: a home, financial security and education for the children.'

"The conventional American dream! Whose convention? What dream? All right then, the choices are these: 1. A home. 2. Financial security. 3. Children.

"Now what do you choose?"

That writer summarized well the problem facing most young couples. They have three alternatives and can afford only one or two at most. As a result, they typically make some serious financial mistakes.

Common Mistakes

The first common mistake is for the wife to work so they can buy their first home or consumer items they think they need. In the next chapter, we'll illustrate "the myth of the working wife," but it can be summarized by saying that it rarely pays for a young mother to work.

You may be thinking, *We don't have children yet.* The problem that often arises, however, is that while you're still childless, you become dependent on two incomes. You find you both need to work to buy the things you're used to buying, and especially to buy that first home. Then, when children come, your financial needs are even greater. Yet statistics show a working mother rarely contributes much to the family's bottom line after all the extra expenses (like child care) are deducted (see chap. 7 for more details).

The second common mistake is falling into the debt mentality. Small charges for things like clothes, travel, home furnishings and eating out have a way of adding up if the bill isn't paid in full each month. Car payments can become a major problem. It's very common for parents to "buy" their adult children a first car by making the down payment and then "giving" them the payment book.

As mentioned before, about 20 percent of disposable income goes toward the repayment of installment and credit card debt. That means that if a couple tithes and pays their taxes and has a 20 percent debt burden, less than 50 percent of their income is available to spend and save for the future. No wonder debt is such a problem for young marrieds!

The third common mistake of young couples is thinking they need to own a home. In the past, a home was a good investment because inflation and low fixed

Small charges for things like clothes, travel, home furnishings and eating out have a way of adding up.

mortgage rates were seemingly guaranteed. In many areas of our country today, however, neither rising home values nor low fixed rates are assured. This might sound harsh, but the American dream of owning a home may have to be given up.

The fact is that young marrieds face the difficult choices pointed out in Sylvester's article. It may not be possible to have a home, children *and* financial security—especially if you don't follow the principles outlined in part 1.

Delayed gratification is absolutely critical to the success of young couples. It's nothing more than waiting to buy something until the money has been saved to pay for it. Instant gratification, on the other hand, is paying whatever price is necessary, including debt, to satisfy some desire *now*. Delayed gratification is a principle taught throughout the Scriptures, especially in the book of Proverbs, whereas instant gratification is never recommended. The Bible says there's a long time between sowing and reaping, and saving for future needs and desires typically requires a long-term perspective.

How to Get Started

Your marriage will start on a much sounder foundation if you follow a few general principles. First, as the wedding vows indicate, becoming husband and wife means that money and possessions are no longer "his" and "mine" but are now "ours." The two of you have become one. It isn't *your* income, *your* savings account, *your* home, *your* car, *your* debt or *your* anything. Neither is it *his* income, *his* home, *his* investments, *his* car or *his* debt. *Any selfish attitude regarding money or possessions will undermine the relationship*—we guarantee it. You may even want to commit everything you have to each other formally so there's no doubt you hold everything jointly.

We know this is an area that involves strong feelings. As one young wife said, "My husband has a bad credit history, but I do not. Should I throw my lot in with his financially or keep stuff separate like I do now? He often resents my earning ability, yet I feel it's my lifeline!" Her feelings are understandable, but she's pursuing financial security at the expense of her marriage, and she may end up with neither.

If you have or expect an inheritance, the principle is the same: it belongs as much to your husband as it does to you. We've seen far too many cases where the husband's authority and ability to provide for the family—even his need to do so—were undermined by his wife's inheritance that had strings attached.

We do not recommend prenuptial agreements or maintaining separate ownership of property, either. If you don't have enough confidence in your husband to give him joint ownership and responsibility, why did you marry him in the first place? We also believe God has promised to meet your needs, and no amount of money in the bank will ever be adequate apart from His blessing. Therefore, you can run the risk of giving up that complete ownership.

The second principle as you're getting started is to make sure you're establishing good habits. Those habits are the cornerstones of good financial management described in part 1.

Third, you need to commit, formally and literally, to constant communication. Because financial matters involve our deepest levels of priorities, communicating about them may be the greatest test of your marriage. It will be most difficult if you don't share the same value system and priorities.

Fortunately in our marriage, we've found that we do have a shared value system. However, after twenty-five years together, we still have difficulty communicating about money matters. One of the primary reasons is a common difference between men and women. Ron tends to take the long-term, conceptual viewpoint, and Judy tends to use what we call the checkbook approach; she interprets our financial well-being according to the balance in her checkbook. From Ron's standpoint, however, our financial well-being is determined by the five-year plan he has in place.

A good illustration of this difference is in how we think of our house. While Ron enjoys the comfort of our home, he also views it as a financial decision we made. He thinks about its resale value, how much it costs us to maintain it and so on. To Judy, however, our home is an expression of herself. She would rarely describe it as a financial decision, even though she understands the financial implications of home ownership.

We've had to learn how to communicate effectively regarding our home, because our individual perspectives haven't changed over the years. We still see things differently. What *has* changed over time is the response we immediately make to the other's viewpoint. We've learned that the other person's perspective isn't wrong, just different. Our commitment to work through our problems and communicate has allowed us to reach that mutual understanding based on acceptance of the fundamental differences in our temperaments.

Principles of Financial Success

Much of what we say here will apply to the rest of the book as well (and we'll occasionally refer back to this chapter). However, there's no better time to begin building financial security, which results in financial freedom, than during the early years of marriage. If you start out right, you can avoid a lot of pain and frustration down the road and be miles ahead of most other couples. In the rest of this chapter, then, we want to discuss the following recommendations.

1. Jointly commit your goals to paper.
2. Draft your first will.
3. Establish giving as a priority.
4. Follow the sequential investing strategy outlined in chapter 17.

5. Get out of and avoid the use of debt.
6. Set up and follow a family budget.
7. Avoid foolish tax-planning decisions.
8. Establish a life insurance program.
9. Decide wisely about purchasing your first home.

Commit Your Goals to Paper

In chapter 3, we talked about the skill of goal setting. When committed to paper, goals provide a strong basis of communication. When they're ill defined, it's difficult for two people to discuss them. So as a couple, you need to determine jointly where you're heading and then write down those goals. When that's done, you've taken the first step toward eliminating potential conflict and controversy.

Would you ever dream of going on a vacation without first determining your destination? Probably not. Otherwise, the husband might start out for the beach, only to have the wife turn the car around and head for the mountains when it's her time to drive. The obvious result would be a lot of conflict.

The need for financial goals is similar. And putting your goals on paper commits the two of you to joint goals. Rather than having goals be "mine" or "yours," they become *our* goals.

Your goals as a young married couple will tend to be short term and life-style centered: furniture, a home down payment, cars, debt payoff and so on. The long-term goals of financial independence, college education, starting your own business and the like are probably not yet a part of the picture. That's not right or wrong; it's just a function of your stage in life.

One common area of conflict in goal setting is that you, as the wife and future mother, may have a much higher need to establish the home—to buy furniture and so on—than does your husband. He probably wants a nice home, too, but he probably doesn't want it as much as you do. In our experience, men tend to be very career- and long-term-financial-security oriented, and both of those conflict with spending for life-style needs in the short term.

In this area as in all others, some trade-off is needed between your husband's priorities and your own. That's why we recommend strongly that you commit your goals jointly to paper. It helps you avoid struggling for superiority in the relationship.

Remember that when you set your goals, they need to be quantified as to time and amount so that they're truly goals and not just broad intentions or purposes.

Periodically throughout the year (perhaps every other month), review your goals to see if they still apply and to check your progress in meeting them. At the very minimum, review your goals annually. Remember that life itself is a dynamic process. What was practical or desirable a year ago may not be the same today. If a goal shows up regularly on your list over time without ever being accomplished, it probably means the goal isn't a high priority with you. Not all goals have the same priority, nor should they.

The process of successful goal setting always begins with prayer to our heavenly Father, who promises in James 1:5 to give wisdom to those who ask. After you pray, each partner should write out all the goals that come to his or her mind—without much thought beforehand—on a blank sheet of paper. Don't worry about wording or anything else. Just record the thoughts and impressions that come to your minds.

Second, each of you should individually consolidate similar goals and eliminate those that aren't really goals but purpose statements. You should then be left with measurable goals.

Third, come together as a couple and discuss, refine and prioritize the goals so that as you enter the next year, you know specifically what you're trying to accomplish and have committed it to paper jointly.

Draft Your First Will

It may seem silly to draft a will right after getting married, especially when you're fairly young and don't expect to die for many years. One of the reasons for having a will, however, is that while it's certain you *will* die, it's very uncertain *when* that will happen. Drafting a will forces you to deal with some issues that only become important after death, when it's too late to do anything about them. It also forces you, as a couple, to discuss your thoughts about dying or surviving your spouse.

The unfortunate fact of the matter is that 70 percent of married women will experience widowhood, and the average age of a widow is fifty-two. One reason the average is so low is that some husbands do die young.

Some of the issues to be decided in drafting a will at an early age arise out of the possibility (unlikely, to be sure, but possible) that you could both die at the same time. In that case, who would be trustee of your property? Who would invest and manage the assets that are left? Who might you want as guardians for your children when they come along? Drafting a will forces discussion of these issues and begins a process of communication that should go on for as long as you both live.

If you should survive your husband, you need to know what his intentions would be relative to your financial life. Does he have certain property he would like to go to a brother or other family member? What does he think you should do in the area of money management and the wealth that might be taken into another marriage? This is an issue that few couples discuss, yet women have to deal with it regularly.

Judy's father died at age forty-two and, as a doctor, left a lot of property to her mother. She remarried after a few years and was married for another fifteen years when she died. The property she had brought into the marriage and that the two of them had accumulated was left basically to her second husband. After two years of being a widower, he married a woman who had also been married previously.

You can see the complexity of the situation, and unless you and your husband discuss these issues before he dies, you won't know how he would want them decided. It's good to know what his wishes are.

One other thing that tends to be discussed when wills are drafted is funeral desires. Again, young couples don't often talk about this topic, though they should. Drafting your will forces you to hold that discussion.

A will never takes effect until the person who drafted it dies, so it can be changed at any time until then. It's a flexible and dynamic document that a good lawyer can craft to meet your unique needs and desires. Nonetheless, one of the big barriers people face in drafting a will is that they don't like to make tough, "final" decisions. But the unavoidable fact is that unless the Lord returns first, you and your spouse *will* die, and if the one who dies doesn't leave an up-to-date will, the survivor will surely regret it.

Establish Giving as a Priority

Ron's firm often works with professional athletes, helping them plan and manage their finances. He remembers visiting once with a young athlete who had just signed a new and very lucrative contract. He was a Christian and desired to do things in a godly manner. When Ron completed his financial analysis, he told the young man he could not only tithe his income, but he could also easily afford to give significantly more. He responded, "I'm making too much money to give. I only have this one-time opportunity to earn this kind of income, and therefore I can't tithe."

That story is applicable to young marrieds because when you first get married these days, you're almost always living on two incomes. Additionally, you have the priorities of buying furniture, saving for a home down payment, paying off debt, buying cars, and so on, all of which conflict with giving. When you stop to think about it, in other words, it's difficult to give when you have larger incomes. As a result, many young couples fail to establish giving as a high priority.

What you need to realize is that there's *no* time when giving will be easy economically. Giving is a spiritual decision made in obedience to God's Word regardless of how easy it is or is not to part with the money. If you wait until you *feel* like giving, you probably never will.

We recommend that young couples, like everyone else, follow 1 Corinthians 16:2 and Proverbs 3:9-10. Give out of the firstfruits on a weekly basis as God has prospered you.

One dilemma young, married women sometimes face was stated clearly by the wife who asked us, "What do you do if your husband doesn't share your concern for tithing?" The women may also have been raised by their parents to give, whereas their husbands weren't taught to make it a high priority. Further, young husbands, with the long term in view, may see giving as a threat to long-term financial security. If any of these apply to your situation, our counsel is to support and encourage your husband to give, but don't demand it.

In our case, Judy became a Christian two years before Ron. At that point, there was no way he was going to give other than to some charity that might benefit his business. And never once during those two years did Judy demand that he tithe their income, even though she felt the need to do so. She just prayed for him and tried to exhibit a 1 Peter 3 life-style, which ultimately became so convicting that

Ron had to deal with the reality of Christ in her life. Had she demanded that he follow her conviction on giving, he probably wouldn't even have been willing to look realistically at the claims of Christ.

Follow the Sequential Investing Strategy

This period of your life is your first great window of financial opportunity. You don't have children yet, you're probably both working, and you haven't yet locked yourselves into big payments for a house or other big-ticket items. Your expenses are lower than they'll ever be. It may not seem that way because of the purchase of furniture, appliances and so on, but believe us, once you have children and you increase your life-style, you'll never again be in as good a financial situation as you are right now.

Young couples typically become dependent upon two incomes. They incur heavy debt loads because they can "afford it." As the cars and furniture depreciate in value and the vacations are gone, however, the debt used to pay for them remains. Consequently, rather than improving their life-style, young couples are actually sentencing themselves to a *lower* standard of living in the future.

The second real window of opportunity doesn't occur until after the children have left and couples are in the empty-nest period. That may be twenty to thirty years before they have significant flexibility in their financial situation again.

Thus, you'll be doing yourself a tremendous favor if you avoid that typical pattern and take advantage of this young-married period to begin a savings program. Specifically, we recommend the sequential investment strategy outlined in chapter 17. This assumes, of course, that you've set up a budget and are generating a positive cash flow monthly or at least annually.

Judy's youngest brother and sister-in-law both went to work for IBM right out of college and got married a couple of years later. They were childless for seven years, and about that time we were discussing their financial condition. They said they had always participated in the IBM savings and stock purchase plans to the maximum amount possible. As a result, in just a few short years they had accumulated a large amount of savings and IBM stock; that provided them a fair degree of financial security and allowed them to purchase their first home.

Company-sponsored savings and stock purchase plans are an excellent way to invest, even if it's just for a short while until you change jobs or stop working to have children. And as Judy's brother said, such plans are a relatively easy way to save, "because money you don't see, you never miss."

IRAs are another good savings vehicle, especially for young couples, whether or not they're tax deductible (it depends on your income and whether you're covered by a pension plan). Figures 5.1 and 5.2 in the previous chapter show the advantage of participating in an IRA at the earliest age possible. (See pp. 53-54.) Where to invest in IRAs is also covered in chapter 17.

Avoid the Use of Debt

Our counsel regarding debt is very simple. First, get out of any debt you already have. Second, avoid the use of credit card, consumer or installment debt in the future. This will mean living within your income and using credit cards only for convenience, paying the balance in full each month. It will also mean saving ahead for all major purchases. Follow the sequential investment strategy and the financial principles in chapter 3.

The Debt Squeeze has chapters on car loans and home mortgages if you want more-detailed information on those types of debt.

Set Up and Follow a Budget

In the last chapter, we described how to establish a budget. (See pp. 58-60.) This chapter focuses on controlling a budget when two people either spend out of the same account or have separate checkbooks and bank accounts.

You and your husband will have to design your own system, but it should include the following five principles so you'll spend only what your income allows according to a predetermined plan.

1. Assigned accountability. Each of you needs to have your own areas of budget responsibility. Someone needs to be in charge of paying the utilities and the rent or mortgage. Someone else may be in charge of the food, clothes and entertainment budget. You both might be responsible for gifts, vacations and so on. It's not important who has what responsibility but rather that each of you understands what your accountability is for the budget. We recommend you go through the budget worksheet and put your initials by the items for which you're responsible. Your husband should do the same. For those items in which you share responsibility, indicate the amount controlled by each.

2. Immediate feedback on how actual spending compares to planned spending. This is similar to operating out of a cookie jar or an envelope. When the envelope or cookie jar is empty, you should stop spending. Your system, whether it involves a check register, literal envelopes or another system you design, should likewise give you immediate feedback on how you stand against your plan. Judy has a budget amount for which she's responsible in our family, and she enters that in her checkbook at the beginning of the month. She can look in her register at any time and tell how she's doing relative to our original plan.

3. Strict limitation of credit card use. Credit cards should be handled just like checks. When cards are used, they're entered in your check register as a check would be. Under the check number you merely put Visa, Mastercard or whatever card you use. Then you fill in the store at which the card was used and the amount, which is deducted from your bank balance just as if you'd written a check. That way, you're effectively setting aside the money to pay the account balance in full at the end of the month.

4. Accumulation of all excess income. If money is not spent by the end of the month, it should be put into a savings account or some other type of account (such as a money market fund) that can be used to make planned purchases. It can even be used as a reward fund. Understand, however, that this is money left over only after you've paid all your bills, including taking savings or investing out of your cash flow as a first priority. If you've already done that, the excess left in the checkbook really is underspending that can be used as you desire.

5. Flexibility. It will take at least two years of living on a budget before you feel comfortable with it. Once the budget has been established and lived with, however, living within your income is extremely easy. But because circumstances change, a budget must be flexible. If you find you budgeted too low or too high in an account, the budget can be adjusted during the year.

As we said in the last chapter and throughout this book, living according to a plan that's God-given and therefore consistent with biblical principles will result in financial freedom. The budget is just one part of effective stewardship.

Avoid Foolish Tax-Planning Decisions

Because of the combination of two incomes, your taxes will probably go up dramatically when you marry. As a result, young couples always wonder how to reduce taxes, and it's for tax reasons that many begin to consider buying a home.

It's true that interest on a home mortgage and property taxes are deductible on your tax return and therefore serve to reduce taxes. However, both mortgage interest and property taxes cost cash out of pocket, so buying a home solely for tax purposes is a poor decision. Instead, you buy a home for reasons revolving around your life-style, recognizing that decision has tax consequences.

Individual retirement accounts or pension plans function both as savings and as a means to reduce taxes, and therefore they make good sense in tax planning.

Increasing charitable giving will also reduce taxes, but that decision, just like taking on home mortgage interest, will cost more money than it saves in taxes.

Be leery of making any financial decision just to reduce your income taxes. As pointed out in the last chapter, the only ways to reduce income tax are to reduce your income or increase your deductible expenses, both of which take money out of your pocket.

As we also said in the last chapter, set your withholdings on your W-4 form so that when your tax return is prepared, the taxes due are as close as possible to the amount withheld from both of your paychecks. (In other words, you don't want to owe anything, but you also shouldn't get money back.) A tax refund is a sign of poor planning; it means you've loaned *your* money to the government all year, interest-free.

Establish a Life Insurance Program

Four basic questions must be answered relative to life insurance. First, "Why have life insurance?" Second, "How much should we have?" Third, "How long will we need it?" Fourth, "What kind of policy is the best to buy?"

You have life insurance to provide for the certainty of death and the possibility that it will happen before you've reached some long-term goals. The life insurance industry euphemistically calls it "premature death." As young married couples, assuming both of you are working, the survivor would no doubt be able to continue working if one of you died. Therefore, you need very little life insurance in this season—enough to cover school and other debts, plus burial expenses.

If you can afford whole-life insurance at this stage, however, you might want to consider it anyway, because such insurance will never be cheaper, and you can lock in a lower payment for life. As you get older, insurance companies will be taking on more risk, so the cost of coverage will go higher and higher.

What kind of insurance to buy is largely an economic question. Whole-life policies initially cost far more than term policies for the same amount of protection, but they have level premiums. Term policies have variable premiums depending on the type of policy, and those premiums go up over time, but they're significantly lower than whole-life premiums in the early years of the policy.

We recommend you determine how much coverage you need and then purchase the least-costly insurance you can. It may be that if you're going to need insurance for a long time, the least-costly coverage (in terms of total premiums paid) is a whole-life policy. If you'll need coverage only for a shorter time (e.g., ten to fifteen years), term insurance is probably the best to buy at this age.

Economic conditions in your area and your unique job situation may be the two most important factors in deciding whether to rent or buy.

Whether you as a wife should be covered by life insurance is also an economic question. You and your husband need to ask yourselves what would happen to his financial situation in the event of your death. If he's dependent on your income, your life should be insured. In most cases, however, that's not the case and life insurance is not needed on your life. Please don't interpret this as saying you're not valuable or important. Of course you are. But spending hard-earned money when it's not really necessary doesn't make sense. This is strictly an economic issue, not a question of your worth. See chapter 15 for a fuller discussion of life insurance.

Decide Wisely about Buying a Home

Most young people want to experience the pride of home ownership as soon as possible, even though it means weekends spent mowing the grass, fixing leaky faucets and so on. The home also lends security to a marriage relationship, which young women greatly appreciate.

In the past few years, high inflation and interest rates have pushed the price of homes out of the reach of many beginning home buyers. Even so, creative financing, equity-sharing arrangements and the like have made it possible for young couples to purchase their first home. However, several issues should be considered before rushing into that decision.

You've probably heard the myth that renting is simply throwing money down the drain, whereas the purchase of a home is the only smart way to provide housing. That may have been true in the past, but it isn't necessarily true today or in the future. Economic conditions in your area and your unique job situation may be the two most-important factors in deciding whether to rent or buy.

Our first recommendation is that you follow the sequential investment strategy to step 4, where you're saving for long-term goals, including home ownership. It's best to save at least 20 percent of the projected price of a home before you purchase. We know this may be difficult or even impossible, and we're not saying you shouldn't buy with a lesser down payment. The greater the down payment, however, the less costly the mortgage will be. Once again, we're dealing with the biblical principle of delayed gratification.

Ron's firm has done a lot of analysis for specific individuals on the buy-versus-rent decision, and we've found that you're better off renting unless you can live in a home for at least two years. That's why it's important to consider your vocational situation.

Second, the more a house costs, the longer you must live in it to make it cheaper than renting. The reason is that many incidental, upfront costs come with home ownership: loan closing costs, new furniture, fix-up costs and so on. The higher the costs, the longer it takes to recover them. So while buying a home remains the American dream, use wisdom in deciding whether it's best for you and whether this is the right time.

If you've decided that now is a good time to give serious thought to home buying, we'd like to give you an overview of things to consider in making a wise choice. The following article appeared in a recent issue of our firm's newsletter, and since it was written by a young married woman (Wendy L. Morgan, a member of our staff) about buying her first home, we thought it best to let you hear directly from her.

"Buying a home can be an intimidating experience, especially the first time. It involves so many decisions! But the following guidelines will help you to avoid most pitfalls in finding and purchasing a home.

"Once you've made the decision to buy, your first consideration is money: How much do you have, and how much can you borrow? The answers to those two questions will control the location and price range of your home.

"The best way to buy a home is to pay cash, but most home buyers must arrange financing. Proverbs 22:7 tells us that the borrower becomes the servant of the lender, so use restraint and proceed cautiously when borrowing.

"Many types of loans are available. Most are arranged through banks and lending institutions, but it's possible to finance a home through the seller or other private individuals. In either case, the terms of the loan will specify the minimum down payment, interest rate, length of loan, repayment terms and qualifying criteria.

"The interest rate can be 'fixed,' meaning it remains the same during the entire loan period, or 'adjustable' or 'variable,' meaning it can change. Adjustable rates are generally tied to some standard interest rate index, such as the current rate on U.S. Treasury bills, and can move up or down. Adjustable rates are initially lower than fixed rates. Since the rate on a loan directly affects the principal and interest payments, adjustable rate mortgages attract buyers who expect their incomes to increase in future years but who initially need lower house payments than current fixed rate loans allow.

"The length, repayment terms and qualifying criteria of a loan can vary. Some loans are repaid with bimonthly [i.e., twice a month] payments, and others are repaid in full at the end of a certain period (i.e., a 'balloon' note). Most are set up for fifteen or thirty years with monthly payments. The length and repayment terms affect the payment amounts and the total amount of interest paid over the life of the loan. Qualifying criteria are the guidelines a lender uses to assess the purchaser's ability to repay the loan.

"To determine how much a person is 'qualified' to borrow, a lender compares the gross monthly income of the applicant(s) to the monthly loan payments. If the 'ratio' of income to debt falls within the qualifying ratios, the lender generally grants the loan. Lenders will also consider credit history and employment stability before approving the loan.

"To illustrate how qualifying ratios are used, let's assume a young couple with a combined yearly income of $36,000 is looking for a home. That income divided by twelve gives a gross monthly income of $3,000. If they apply for a loan that requires a 10 percent down payment and has qualifying ratios of 28 percent and 36 percent, their down payment must be 10 percent of the purchase price, their monthly house payment (principal, interest, taxes and insurance) cannot exceed 28 percent of their gross income ($840), and their house payment plus all other debt payments (e.g., car notes, credit cards, etc.) cannot exceed 36 percent of their gross income ($1,080).

"Figure 6.1 will help you find your price range, as well as illustrate how interest rates affect the monthly principal and interest payments. Determine the maximum monthly house payment you can afford, then look at the chart to see how much you can borrow at the various interest rates.

Figure 6.1

MONTHLY PAYMENTS

Loan Amount	Interest Rate		
	9%	10%	11%
$ 70,000	$ 564	$ 615	$ 667
$ 80,000	644	702	762
$ 90,000	725	790	858
$100,000	805	878	953
$125,000	1,006	1,098	1,191

"Another way to determine your price range is to speak with a loan officer. Most lenders offer a prequalifying interview at no charge, which is an excellent way to learn about loans, closing costs and prepaid items involved in purchasing a home.

"Closing costs and prepaid items are in addition to the down payment and include such things as points paid for the privilege of getting a loan (one point is 1 percent of the loan amount), appraisal fees, prepaid property taxes, attorneys' fees and on and on. You need to check with a loan officer or real estate agent about the specific costs for which you will be responsible.

"Now that you have a general understanding of financing and your price range, you can realistically begin listing and prioritizing your housing needs and wants. The wants and needs of people differ greatly, but whether you're interested in single family housing or condominiums, you can venture out on your own or contact a real estate agent.

"Real estate agents are state-licensed and trained in basic financing and writing purchase contracts. They can usually show and sell homes offered for sale, or 'listed,' by other agents as well as their own listings, even those listed by other companies. A good agent will answer your questions and make suggestions based on your needs and wants."

Conclusion

Establishing your marriage on sound financial principles is one of the most important decisions you'll ever make. Many first-time decisions about buying a home, paying off debt, saving for the future, buying life insurance and so on make this a critical period. If you can get started right, you'll minimize conflict in one of the most sensitive areas of marriage. Your role as a wife will probably never be tested more.

We say that because most men, no matter how successful, lack training and expertise in making sound financial decisions for a family. Therefore, your ability to communicate with your husband will determine, to a large extent, his feelings of self-worth in this area. It's a tremendous challenge. As we indicated earlier, you will probably be a good intuitive decision maker, which will go against his logical approach to financial decisions. If you can establish the right habits and the right communication process at this stage of your marriage, you will have been blessed abundantly.

CHAPTER SEVEN

Two Incomes or One: Young Children

Our youngest child, Michael, was born in 1978. His oldest sister, Cynthia, was eleven; Denise was nine; Karen was six; and Tim was three. We were thirty-six (Ron) and thirty-four (Judy).

We were involved in full-time ministry, and Ron was traveling extensively. He had left his CPA business a year earlier, and we were right in the center of God's will. At that age and stage of our life together, we should have had the most vitality we'd ever enjoyed. We had been through enough as a married couple to have worked out many of the problems, and we had five lovely children. Financially we were in sound shape, with no real worries. Yet one day at the office, Ron got a call from Judy, and during the conversation she said, "If this is the abundant life Jesus talks about in John 10:10, it isn't very abundant."

What she meant was that she was physically exhausted. All her decisions tended to be short term in perspective, and they were always at someone else's demand. To try to get her to sit down and talk about our long-term goals would have been laughable. Her long-term goal was to make it to the end of the day without collapsing under the stress and strain of managing five children.

Since then, as we have counseled other couples with young children, we've found physical exhaustion and short-term perspective to be characteristic of that age. Additionally, many young couples have to adjust to one income and have difficulty saving any money. The money they do save can create conflict because of the different needs a husband and wife have.

In the national survey conducted for this book, the number one concern of women in this season of life was making ends meet. A recent *Wall Street Journal* article brought this home to us. It was datelined Milwaukee and said: "Economist Edward Yardeni sees the future rich with the savings of graying baby boomers. But has he talked to the folks in this brick-and-beer heartland city?"

The article went on to describe two young couples (the Dudeks and Pitterles) in which the husbands have well-paying jobs, yet they're struggling to make ends meet. Neither couple is able to save much for future needs. "Messrs. Dudek and Pitterle are concerned about their level of savings, and they are trying . . . to salt away some extra dollars. But so far, they aren't salting away enough to lend much support to Mr. Yardeni's forecast. And overall, Americans are notoriously poor savers. Although the personal-savings rate jumped one percentage point last year to 4.2% of after-tax income, that is still a far cry from the rates in Japan and much of Europe."

Financial Impact of Children

It may seem as if your children cost you a great deal, but having raised five and counseled other parents, we can assure you that "you ain't seen nuthin' yet." The average cost to raise a child to age eighteen is at least $100,000. If that child then decides to go to college, the additional cost can be anywhere from $20,000 to another $100,000.

When you consider those figures, the cost of raising children seems to dictate the mother must work outside the home. Yet the need and desire to provide nurture calls for the opposite. An article in the *Los Angeles Times* of August 12, 1990, by Lynn Smith and Bob Sipchen showed just how much modern parents struggle with that conflict.

"Haunted by anxiety about too little time with their children, nearly 40% of fathers and 80% of mothers in Los Angeles and Orange counties say they would quit their jobs, if they could, to rear their children at home.

"Most parents say they are often overwhelmed by the responsibilities of child-rearing and worry about whether they are doing a good job of it, according to a Los Angeles Times-commissioned survey of 1,000 households in the two counties.

"Some social historians say the findings reflect a 'new realism' about the financial and emotional toll that an 80-hour work week inflicts on dual-earner families.

"'We've reached a time when we're more realistic of what the costs are of full-time employment for two-earner families,' said Barbara Dafoe Whitehead, a social historian and consultant with the Chicago-based Public Policy Assn. The two top responsibilities of parenthood—providing financial security and passing on values—are on a collision course that will continue at least through the decade or until the economy eases, she said" (copyright 1990, *Los Angeles Times;* reprinted by permission).

As we pointed out in the last chapter, providing financial security for a family, buying a home and raising children are just too much for many families today. It may be that only one or two of those objectives can realistically be met.

What to Do

We don't want to paint an entirely pessimistic picture, however. Peace of mind is possible for couples raising young children if they daily do things right, maintain a long-term perspective and continue to believe God's principles are working. Hope can be hard to come by at this time of life, but you *will* get through it.

As always, financial success begins with adherence to the cornerstones outlined in chapters 2 and 3. In addition, several key concerns will require your attention during this period of your life; we'll look at them in this chapter.

First, the right life insurance now becomes essential because you have young children. Second, at some point a larger home may be needed as the children get older. (Home buying is covered in detail in chap. 6.) Third, your will definitely should be revised, probably every other year. Fourth, your short-term spending plans become critical, as there's very little surplus and maybe only one income. Fifth, long-term goals, while still important, are realistically not urgent. Sixth, you'll want to train your children in managing money so they start out on a sound footing (a responsibility neglected by most parents).

We also need to address the financial implications of a working mother, as 60 percent of the Christian women in our survey work outside the home at least part-time. No doubt the other 40 percent wonder whether they've made the right decision, as they feel tremendous financial pressure.

Before we get to those areas, however, we need to look briefly at how some of the financial basics apply specifically to this season of life. We begin by considering giving to the Lord.

Giving

For the next several years, you and your husband will be sorely tempted to reduce or defer your charitable giving. The demands of children and establishing a household make this an obvious area to cut, as there are no apparent personal consequences.

However, as we pointed out in chapter 2 and elsewhere throughout this book, giving is a spiritual decision and will come only from the spiritual conviction that God owns it all. Tithing on your gross income is recognition of His ownership and an expression of trust in His provision for your needs (but not necessarily all your wants). It also helps you set proper priorities in the other areas of your financial life. Our recommendation, therefore, is that you never look at reducing your tithe as a way to free up money for other things.

Ron has counseled thousands of young couples over the last several years, and he has yet to meet a couple who began their marriage by making the tithe a habit and who had financial problems. That's not to say they had a surplus of money so they could do whatever they wanted, but their needs were met. God honors His Word, and His Word is clear that giving should be the first priority use of our money.

Saving

Following the sequential investment strategy outlined in chapter 17 is especially critical during this period. You should have monies set aside for emergencies, because as your children get older and you establish your home, the unexpected expenses will come more frequently. If you don't have emergency funds set aside, those expenses can cause major stress in your marriage.

You also want to continue funding retirement and savings plans. This is the ideal time of life to begin setting aside money for your children's college education. For example, if at a child's birth you started depositing $100 per month in a savings account for his or her education, you would have deposited $21,600 by the time the child turns eighteen. However, through the magic of compounding, if that money had earned an average of 12 percent per year (which is not unrealistic), you would have accumulated $75,786 toward that college education (before taxes). That would pay for four years at almost any college in America today. (It may not in eighteen years, but it would today.)

If you made a one-time deposit of $5,000 at birth and it grew at 12 percent compounded annually, the fund would be worth $42,893 (before taxes) at the end of eighteen years.

There are many ways to save regularly for college education. Mutual funds offer investment programs in which your bank account can be drafted each month for a certain amount—as low as $50, depending on the fund. If you start early and have an eighteen-year perspective, you'll be able to weather the ups and downs of market cycles, and many funds have exceeded 12 percent annual return over a long time period.

Company savings plans and whole life insurance policies bought for the child at birth can also be good alternatives for college savings. The real issue is not so much the investment vehicle as it is the discipline of saving. You won't give up today's desires for future benefits unless you have a long-term perspective.

By making these recommendations, we're not saying that every child has to go to college or that you should pay for 100 percent of your children's college education. What we *are* saying is that if you want your children to go to college and you want to pay for that, starting early is the easiest way to do it. Waiting until kids are college age is extremely difficult.

We speak from great experience, having five children times four years each in college—twenty years of college education—to fund. That twenty years of college will be paid for over about fifteen years. To wait until our children were in college to begin saving for that education might have eased financial pressures in the short term, but it would have compounded the pressure in the long term.

Use of Debt

Debt will become a great temptation as you face the financial pressures of this period, since it appears to be an easy way to meet short-term needs and desires. In almost every chapter of this book, however, we've warned about the dangers of debt. The long-term costs are bondage and potential financial failure. Borrowing obligates you many years into the future to make payments on that amount.

If you use credit cards, for example, and only make the minimum payment each month, you'll probably be covering little more than the new interest cost, leaving the principal largely untouched. We can only say that avoiding debt still makes good sense.

Family Budget

By now your budget is beginning to reflect the costs of children. Their schooling, clothes, entertainment, sports and so on are obvious expenses. The indirect costs in such things as housing, food and family vacations are more difficult to measure.

We recommend you begin training your kids to manage money at a fairly early age—perhaps as young as five years old. By age eight or ten, they can usually be given responsibility for managing *their* portion of *your* budget: money for their

Children learn responsibility by having responsibility.

clothes, their lunches, their personal spending, the gifts they give to others and any other direct items of expense you're now paying for them.

We've written a book called *Raising Money-Smart Kids* dealing with the whole process of training children to manage money. The primary point is that children learn responsibility by having responsibility, and you can both train them and help your own family budget by giving them the responsibility to manage, according to a system, the portion of the family budget they're spending.

It's been our observation that the primary trainer of children in managing money is their mother. Your role in this regard is probably the most significant influence they'll ever have. The value system you pass down is the one they'll take into their own marriages and pass on to their own children. Being a mother is an awesome but usually thankless job, with few immediate rewards. But here again, we encourage you to take a long-term, biblical perspective, drawing on the Lord's strength and wisdom and looking forward to hearing His "Well done."

Life Insurance

You may feel like the mother who asked, "Is all this life insurance really necessary when Johnny needs braces *now?*" We can appreciate the feeling because of the tightness of the family budget in this stage of life, but adequate life insurance is never more important than when you have young children. You want to make sure you have enough insurance on the primary breadwinner to cover all needs arising from his death. This would include mortgage debt and a college fund for your children.

If you're not working outside the home and don't plan to do so in the event of your husband's death, there also needs to be enough insurance to create an investment fund that will provide enough income that you can be financially independent. This may seem like a huge amount of insurance, and it is, but term insurance can be provided at a low cost to meet all these needs.

Chapter 15 discusses life insurance in much greater detail, but your action step at this point is to make sure you have adequate coverage.

Should you insure your children? There are three reasons to consider it: (1) to guarantee them insurability as they get older should they have an accident or illness that would otherwise make them uninsurable; (2) to set up a long-term savings program for them, perhaps to fund college education; (3) to pay for burial expenses should they die (normally $2,000-$5,000). This last expense may be covered best by a rider on your own policy.

Wills

The birth of children calls for an updating of your wills, and the three most important decisions to be made at this point have nothing to do with money. Instead, you need to prayerfully consider the following three appointments.

1. Executor. Husbands and wives typically name each other as their executors. The executor is responsible for assembling the property belonging to the estate, safeguarding and insuring the property during the period of the estate settlement, managing the estate while it's being settled, paying estate taxes and expenses, accounting for the estate administration and making distribution of the net estate to the heirs.

The duties of the executor can be time consuming, frustrating and complicated. As a surviving spouse, you may find them overwhelming. But when you need assistance, a financial counselor, bank or attorney can help. In the event that you and your husband should die at the same time, your wills should name some qualified individual or corporate trust company as executor.

The job of executor is temporary, ending when the estate is distributed.

2. Trustee. If some of your estate is left in trust, you'll need a trustee. This person is responsible for managing the estate according to the terms of the will and making distributions accordingly. Either an individual or corporation (e.g., a bank) may be the trustee. We typically recommend having an individual trustee—again, usually your spouse. If a corporate trustee is named, the surviving spouse should have the right to replace that trustee, as institutions change over time.

3. Guardian. We've saved the most important decision for last. The guardian must be someone you would feel comfortable leaving your children with to raise them if both of you were to die. Consideration should be given to the financial situation of the potential guardian, his or her health, age, spiritual maturity and the compatibility of his or her values with yours.

We have changed guardians many times over the course of our marriage. Our values have changed, especially after we became Christians, and the circumstances and friendships with guardians selected have changed.

Early in our marriage, we chose relatives. But as relatives had their own responsibilities or grew older, it became impractical to use them. We then began to choose friends. As we've moved around the country, and as our friends and our values have changed, we've changed the guardians in our wills. Now we've reached the stage where our older children are old enough and mature enough to be the guardians of their siblings.

In addition to one primary executor, trustee and guardian, you should select an alternate for each job. You should also discuss the selection with the person or persons chosen before naming them in your wills.

Major Decisions

Women with young children face many major decisions. Three of the most important are whether to send your kids to Christian schools, whether to work outside the home and how to pay for the family vacation.

Christian Schools: An Economic Decision?

Recently Ron counseled a young professional couple whose income was nearly $100,000. They told him they didn't have enough money to tithe, pay off their debt, maintain their life-style and send their children to a Christian school. They wanted his help in moving from a negative to a positive cash flow.

While reviewing their budget, Ron asked if they were willing to move their children into public schools to save money. They told him in no uncertain terms that that was not an option. As Ron reflected on their answer, he realized their private school decision was not economic in nature but rather a priority decision. They were saying that because acceptable public education was not available, one of their highest priorities was to send their kids to private schools.

Ron told them their financial priorities appeared to be, in order of importance: (1) to send their children to private school; (2) to maintain their life-style; (3) to pay their taxes; (4) to pay off their debt; (5) to tithe; and (6) to provide for the future through savings programs. Because of their negative cash flow, they were unable to put money toward the last three priorities at all. (Rather then reducing debt, they were in fact increasing it.) Ron pointed out that the Christian school decision was therefore a priority decision.

If they chose to make private school a high priority and still wanted to tithe, pay off debt, pay their taxes and save for the future, their only option was to reduce their life-style. They simply couldn't continue to live in the same home and neighborhood, take the same vacations, spend as much on entertainment and clothes and so forth. That godly couple realized that in fact it was a priority decision, and they were willing to reduce their life-style to maintain the priorities they felt God would have them follow.

Many decisions we make seem to be strictly financial in nature when they're

*O*nce the priorities of life are set, money becomes nothing more than the tool used to accomplish those priorities.

really priority decisions. Once the priorities of life are set, money becomes nothing more than the tool used to accomplish those priorities. Most people spend a lifetime trying to avoid this simple fact: Unless you have unlimited resources (and no one does), you will never be able to spend as if you do.

When you choose to spend money on one priority such as a Christian school, the money is not available for other priorities. Therefore, you must understand what your top priorities are. And spending on one high priority means other areas of your life may have to be adjusted downward. In other words, you can't have everything.

Working Mother?

The *Los Angeles Times* article of August 12, 1990, referred to earlier in this chapter includes the story of a struggling working mother: "For Benay Clark, facing her 2-1/2-year-old daughter, Mallory, before her husband takes the girl to day care each morning is 'a real struggle.'

"Sometimes, Mallory clings to her; she says she's scared; she asks why Clark has to have a job.

"'I've cried on my way to work many times,' said Clark, a 35-year-old administrative clerk living in the West Hills area of the San Fernando Valley.

"Irene Quintanilla Smith, who runs the child-care center where Mallory spends her days, said she often sees tears on parents' faces as well as children's. Mothers and fathers tell her they 'had a parent home when they were children and they wish they could do the same. But they can't,' because their financial situation forces them to work."

The article goes on to say that 86 percent of the people surveyed agree with Smith that two incomes are necessary. Further, a little more than half the men said their parenting has suffered "a lot" or "some" because of their jobs, and 39 percent of the women said the same. If given the choice, 39 percent of the men said they would stay home to raise their kids, and a full 79 percent of the women would also.

The survey conducted for this book indicated that 60 percent of Christian women work outside the home, and a large majority of them also say the reason is economic necessity. Since that's the case, we need to take a closer look at the real financial consequences of a mother's working.

We developed a chart in our firm to do just that (fig. 7.1). Russ Crosson uses it in his book *Money and Your Marriage,* which has a significant chapter on working mothers. The chart offers some interesting insights.

Some of the expenses that come out of the mother's paycheck are fixed—income taxes, Social Security taxes and the tithe. Others are variable—transportation, meals, clothes, hairdresser, day care and miscellaneous costs.

Local, state and federal income taxes will generally total at least 33 percent of your salary. You can take a tax credit if you have day-care expenses.

Day-care expenses are assumed to be $65 per week per child. This cost will vary from place to place but is most likely a realistic and even conservative average. The other variable expense estimates are normal for each category, but of course each family budget is a little different. What you need to do is not ignore these expenses but measure them realistically.

The eye-opening revelation is that if a working mother has an annual salary of $20,000, *she's contributing less than $2,000 to the family's well-being.* If day care is not used and that $6,200 is therefore saved, she's still contributing less than half her total income (to be precise, $1,978 plus the day care [$6,240] minus the loss of the day care credit of $1,200, for a total of $7,018).

In other words, the working mother is trading 2,000 hours of work per year, plus commuting time, for $7,018 of extra income for the family. That equals $3.51 per hour. If she uses day care, she's contributing *less than $1 per hour to*

Figure 7.1
The myth of the working mother—
what your paycheck is really worth

Annual Salary	$10,000	$20,000	$30,000
Expenses			
Fixed expenses			
Federal income tax (1)	1,500 (15%)	5,600 (28%)	8,400 (28%)
State income tax	600	1,200	1,800
Social Security tax	751	1,502	2,253
Tithe	1,000	2,000	3,000
Day-care credit (2)	(1,440)	(1,200)	(960)
Variable expenses			
Transportation	600	600	600
Meals ($2/day)	480	480	480
Clothing	400	600	800
Hairdresser	300	400	500
Day-care expense (3)	6,240	6,240	6,240
Miscellaneous	600	600	600
Total expenses	11,031	18,022	23,713
Contribution to family income	(1,031)	1,978	6,287

(1) 15% bracket if family taxable income is less than $29,750; over $29,750 is taxed at 28%.
(2) Day-care credit is equal to $720 per child at $10,000 salary level; credit scales down to $480 per child at $30,000 salary level. Credit limited to 2 children.
(3) 2 children at $65 per week.

the family's financial well-being.

The obvious question then becomes whether that money provides enough benefit to warrant what's given up in terms of the relationship with and training of the children. Whether the money is used for financial security, house payments, the children, life-style desires, debt payments, vacations or whatever, is that a good trade-off?

We don't mean to imply there's only one right answer; each woman has to make that determination for herself. But we do want you to understand clearly that earning $20,000 per year does not provide $20,000 of benefit to the family. It more realistically will provide either no benefit at all or perhaps 35 to 40 percent of the gross salary.

The Family Vacation

One of the big financial decisions for young families every year concerns the family vacation: where to spend it, who to spend it with, how to spend it and how to pay for it. The answers to those questions can bring either great enjoyment and togetherness—or frustration and stress.

Some families suffer through their vacations with guilt feelings, thinking they shouldn't be spending so much money. Many families don't even pay off last year's vacation before this year's rolls around. The following five recommendations may help you survive the vacation not only financially, but also in more important ways.

1. Understand your real objectives. Not everything that appears to be a vacation is; it may merely be an activity. When you end your vacation, each family member should be able to say, "Now *that* was a vacation."

A vacation should first provide a break in routine for every member of the family, whether that routine is school, doing dishes, making phone calls or whatever. Therefore, a vacation needs to be long enough to enable each person to unwind from daily activities.

Second, a family vacation should build memories. Whether you go to the beach or travel to different locations every year, you're building memories. Often the difficult times on vacation are remembered the most fondly. All of us Blues remember when it rained all weekend as we were attempting our first camping trip. We thought that only happened in the movies, but it happened to us. We also remember well the three days it took us to drive to Colorado in a small station wagon with five children ages four to fifteen. Today we all laugh at those experiences. At the time they didn't seem so funny, but memories were made.

Our third objective is to build relationships. This means we do things together as a family, but we also have the freedom to go alone. Relationships can't be forced; they must happen. Therefore, the environment selected for the vacation is important.

Other objectives may involve rest, education, visiting family and friends and whatever is unique to your own family and desires.

2. Make the children a part of the whole process. We have always tried to decide where we're going on vacation through family conferences in which we set objectives and priorities, discuss alternatives and establish a budget. This helps us avoid conflict, teaches us how to make decisions and how to work together, and gives goal ownership to each family member.

Children should be encouraged and helped to save money during the year for the vacation. That will allow them the freedom to spend on vacation without the guilt so many parents feel because they can't afford it. Saving to spend also teaches delayed gratification and gives kids a sense of excitement in thinking about the vacation.

Remember, however, to let them spend their vacation money as they wish. They've saved for it and should be allowed to spend pretty much as they see fit. That helps avoid conflict and builds a trust relationship between you and them.

3. Never borrow to pay for a vacation. A vacation budget should be part of your annual spending plan. Then when vacation time arrives, there's no guilt related to spending the money. Stewardship is the use of God's resources to accomplish His purposes, and building family memories and relationships is a legitimate purpose. If the money has been saved ahead of time, you'll experience freedom from guilt, freedom to spend, freedom from financial bondage and freedom from family conflict.

If you haven't been able to save ahead, that doesn't necessarily mean no vacation. It just means a creative alternative is required, which leads to the next recommendation.

4. Be creative in saving money. Can your objectives be accomplished in some way that doesn't cost much? For example, can you camp out instead of staying in a hotel? Can you stay with friends? Can you pack lunches rather than eat out every meal? Costs are lower in some seasons than in others, especially in resort locations. What activities can be done that don't require spending money?

As a last alternative, it may be that the vacation the family really wants must be delayed until a later time, when adequate funds can be accumulated. In the meantime, look for enjoyable things to do closer to home.

5. *Trust God to provide the resources.* Whenever you borrow for a vacation, you're saying in effect that God can't provide your vacation except through a lender. Several years ago, we prepared our annual budget and determined there was no money for a vacation. So we decided to stay home and drive to the lake, go to ball games and so on.

What happened, however, was a demonstration of God's incredible faithfulness. That year we were offered five different vacations for free, one of which was worth several thousand dollars! God provided far beyond what we could have ever done for our family. It taught our family a tremendous lesson regarding God's goodness.

The family vacation should not be a financial, emotional or physical drain on the family, and with proper planning it doesn't have to be.

Conclusion

This time of life, while potentially stressful, will pass far too quickly, and then you'll have nothing to show for it other than the memories and the consequences of the good decisions you've made. Our desire is that you'll be able to look back on this period without guilt or remorse over poor financial decisions.

Trade-offs between the short term and the long term in your planning are inevitable, with the pressures being on the short term. The most important priority is the establishment of your family and beginning the training process with your children. Our prayer is that "God [will] fill you with the knowledge of his will through all spiritual wisdom" (Col. 1:9) so that the decisions you make will be His decisions for you.

CHAPTER EIGHT

Another Coping Gap: Teen and College-Age Children

*I*n the last chapter, we talked about the physical exhaustion that's common in young motherhood. When children get to the teen and college years, the demands on a mother change in nature—they're now more emotional than physical—but they may be even more exhausting.

A mother's problems and decisions become increasingly serious as the children get older. Do you send them to public or private schools? What kind of friendships are they forming, and is their peer group influence positive or negative? Where will they go to college, and who'll pay those bills? Whom will they marry? These issues can be gut wrenching for parents.

A woman has probably been married fourteen to twenty-five years at this point, and communication patterns with her husband are now solidified. If there are barriers to good communication, they will be difficult to overcome—they may seem insurmountable.

As our survey indicated, the ability to live as well in the next period of life as you have in the past becomes very much in doubt. This is due primarily to the tremendous financial needs of this season: college, cars, weddings, travel, trying to get out of debt and so on.

A career change is not at all unusual for the husband at this stage, which is extremely challenging emotionally and mentally. The reason is the crisis many men go through when, at about age forty, they realize their career goals and dreams, and perhaps even dreams for their families, are *not* going to be realized.

Many financial problems common to this time are symptomatic of something else: for example, lack of communication, little self-discipline, no prior planning or poor decision making. The real problem now is that many years have gone by, compounding the problems, and working your way out becomes increasingly difficult.

Without question, raising your children will be your biggest expense. An article in *Money* magazine (July 1990) outlined what it costs.

> You'll spend at least $265,249 to raise him or her to 22 years of age, according to the U.S. Department of Agriculture. That includes housing costs of $84,880, food $61,007, transportation $39,787, clothing $18,567, and medical bills not covered by insurance $18,567. Moreover, economies of scale are minimal. Bringing up two kids will cost you $419,093 (or about $209,546 per child); three and four will run $568,959 and $758,612, respectively. And that's just the base sum. All of the projections assume 6% average annual inflation, except for higher education which calls for 7%.

Those statistics don't include the costs of preschool, music or athletic lessons, private school, child care, summer camp or private college. Attending an Ivy League college could add as much as $300,000 to the total. When you add these costs to those reported in that study, it can easily take $500,000 to $1,000,000 to raise a child born in 1990 through the first twenty-two years of life. The point is that the cost of raising children is significantly more than most of us realize.

Much of what has been said so far assumes that the right building blocks have been put in place for financial success during this stage of life. Even if everything has been done correctly, however, the two big areas that need to be confronted financially are the training of children in money management and the funding of college education. So in this chapter, we'll discuss the major issues that have to be faced (including how to train kids), our recommendations in the various financial planning areas and how to pay for college.

Major Issues Relative to Children

Experience shows there are four major issues with your kids at this stage: training them to manage money responsibly; creating the proper expectations in them regarding what you will and won't do; deciding whether they should work during their high school years; and helping them make their choice of college. We'll deal with them in that order.

Teaching Money Management

To learn how to manage money responsibly, children must have responsibility for managing money. They learn by doing. Our youngest son is a tennis player, and he has begun stringing rackets to pay for some of the extra costs of playing competitive tennis, such as expensive rackets. He's also saving a large sum of money now, at age thirteen, planning to buy a car when he turns sixteen.

This has all been done with no argument, incentive or inducement on our part. Rather, we gave him the responsibility, beginning at about age eight, of managing for himself the amounts we were willing to spend for clothes, spending

> *C*hildren should not leave home without knowing how to manage money, balance a checkbook, use a credit card responsibly and set up a simple budget.

money, lessons and so forth. He has seen that it's necessary to work to get some of the things he would like to have. Therefore, it's been natural for him to begin saving for long-term desires.

Children should not leave home without knowing how to manage money, balance a checkbook, use a credit card responsibly and set up a simple budget.

Creating Proper Expectations

One of the greatest barriers to communication between parents and children is the differences in their expectations. Children may expect, for example, to buy Polo shirts, have new cars when they reach age sixteen, get help from Mom and Dad in acquiring their first homes and so on. Parents, on the other hand, may have no intention of providing all their kids expect. The challenge is to eliminate that barrier by reconciling expectations and reality.

You do that by making your decisions early about what you'll provide in the way of cars, college, help with the first home, weddings and so on. Those can all be major areas of expense for a family. Then communicate your decisions so your children have time to accept the reality.

Our third child began attending a private high school five years ago. The school was in an affluent area, and many of her classmates were expecting to receive brand-new cars when they turned sixteen. It wasn't uncommon for kids to receive a BMW or a Porsche on their birthday.

We had determined we were willing to buy our daughter a car, too. However, because it was being bought for our convenience rather than hers, and because we were the ones buying it, the car would be an inexpensive, used model that would provide her reliable transportation but no glamour. We further said that because it was our car, we would provide the gas for the driving she would do in place of her mother. If she chose to drive the car other than to and from school, she would have to earn the money for the extra gas. Also, because it was our car, we would pay for the insurance. Any traffic violations or damages she incurred would be paid for by her.

We began communicating all this to her when she was thirteen, so she was well settled with the reality of what to expect when she reached sixteen. We had also determined how much we were willing to spend for that car. She could choose the car as long as she stayed within that budget.

Picking the car was tremendously educational for her. She learned how to read the want-ads and how to make a major financial decision. Because she had never made that decision before, we spent a lot of time together talking over the alternatives. Eventually she made an excellent choice, and we noticed that high-priced, new imports were never even mentioned. She was enthusiastic about that inexpensive, used car, and perhaps even more appreciative than her classmates were of more-expensive cars.

By giving her the right expectations and the freedom to choose within them, reality became even better than what she expected. We turned a potentially negative experience into one that was extremely positive.

Another area where we've found it necessary to begin communicating is with regard to what we'll pay for a wedding. Our three oldest children are daughters, so wedding costs could be burdensome to our family. Though none of our daughters are contemplating marriage at this point, they know what to expect when the time comes. As they go to their friends' weddings, they ask questions about what costs what so they can make their own plans more intelligently.

Deciding Whether a Child Should Work

It used to be a foregone conclusion that children would have summer jobs or even work during school. With the increasing affluence of many families, however, that's become less common. But whether a child should have a summer or a part-time job may not be strictly an economic decision; a job may be a good idea just as a means of training.

When J.C. (Jim) Penney, founder of the department store chain, was eight years old, his father told him that as of that moment, he was on his own financially. He now had to make enough money to buy all his clothes and other necessities of life except for food and shelter. At the time Jim had only an old pair of shoes, and he asked his father if he could at least begin with a new pair of shoes. His father said no, he was now on his own, and he would have to make do.

That sounds harsh, but it was his father's apparently sincere best effort to teach Jim the necessity of discipline and responsibility and the reward of work.

Today, teens might work to help pay for their college education or major purchases like a car, as well as just to relieve the boredom that comes during the summer vacation months. It used to be, in an agricultural society, that children *had* to work. In our largely urban society, however, kids with paying jobs are in the minority.

Two *risks* in letting children work also need to be mentioned. One is that they could get out of balance by putting more emphasis on earning money than on schoolwork, church and other healthy activities. Second, they could end up associating with a peer group that has a totally different value system from yours.

These risks need to be understood and watched for, but they're not so great that teens should not have some type of job.

Children today have many summer opportunities—church camp, retreats, sports camps, family vacations—that weren't available to us, our parents or our grandparents. The challenge is to determine ahead of time how work, family vacation and so forth fit into your priorities as a family. It may be that a summer job is impractical because you have higher priorities for your kids. If that's the case, however, you need to provide other opportunities for your children to learn the value of work. That may be around the house or in a part-time job where flexibility in scheduling is possible.

How you make that decision and how it's presented are extremely important; effective communication reduces the likelihood of conflict. Such communication, especially with an adolescent, is explained well in Dr. James Dobson's book *Preparing for Adolescence,* which we heartily recommend.

Choosing a College

The fourth major issue is helping your children choose colleges. (The same approach works with vocational schools or other kinds of training programs.) We have now been through the process three times and have learned that it never gets easier. Each child has unique interests, desires and aptitudes that make the choice difficult.

Choosing a college begins with listing all the things your child wants in a school. Think in terms of school size, location, courses and majors offered, friends, Christian fellowship offered, campus setting, cost and so on. After the criteria are listed, prioritize the list so you keep the most important items foremost in mind as you evaluate different colleges. Don't rule out expensive private schools yet if they meet your other top criteria; your child may be eligible for scholarships.

Next, from as many sources as you can find, list all the colleges you want to consider. Then gather the facts about each school to see how well it meets your criteria and how it compares to the other choices. If this process narrows the choices to less than a handful and your child is still undecided, you may want to visit the schools and sit in on some classes and talk to students.

Finally, choose the college that best meets the prioritized criteria. The result is a well-researched, logical decision rather than one based only on feelings. That doesn't guarantee a perfect choice, but such an objective process increases the chances of making the best one.

Too often we parents try to dictate our kids' college choices based on our

Too often we parents try to dictate our kids' college choices based on our desires rather than their objectives.

desires rather than their objectives. By allowing them to work through the process of this major decision, we build into them one of the most-important skills they can acquire. In fact, since few of *us* were taught how to make a decision, choosing a college can be a tremendous educational experience for both us and our children.

Financial Planning Recommendations

As our children have grown older, the emotional drain has become greater. One way we've found to maintain our perspective is to take a couple of weekends away each year, just the two of us. We've gone to a borrowed mountain cabin, a borrowed beach condominium, and even to a hotel not ten minutes from our house. Those have been ideal times for longer-term financial dreaming and goal setting. We talk, list, talk some more and refine our list. Over time, we've found there are just a few long-term goals that are really high priorities for us. Those weekends give us an opportunity to communicate and determine once again that the goals we're working toward are right for us.

Besides planning, we pray and play together during those weekends. They've become real highlights of our married life, and we recommend such planning weekends for every married couple. They don't have to be expensive, but it's important that you do something like that so you and your husband know where you're headed together.

Giving

The temptation to reduce giving during this time of life becomes almost overwhelming; it seems an easy and obvious way to free up cash.

At best, however, reducing your giving is a short-term solution to your financial pressures. We would remind you of the biblical perspective outlined in chapter 2—God owns it all. Giving as a first priority helps you keep the right priorities in your finances and in your life generally. Those priorities don't change just because your budget is tight, nor does God's faithfulness.

Our recommendation relative to reducing giving is very simple: Don't.

Budget

By now, most of your spending disciplines are in place. Changing old habits is always difficult, but we have two suggestions to help you make sure you're spending the way you want to be. First ask yourself, "Does our use of the income God has entrusted to us continue to reflect proper priorities?" What percent of your income is allocated to giving, saving, debt repayment, life-style and taxes? Are those the priorities you believe God would have for you?

Second, spend time together as a husband and wife each month reviewing where you stand financially. What changes occurred during the month? What are the plans for next month? And again, does your spending reflect the priorities you would like it to reflect?

If you and your husband have trouble communicating about finances, it might be helpful to ask his opinion on certain sections of this book. We're not suggesting that as a sneaky way to get him to read the book. Rather, let him have his say about what this book suggests. Effective communication is critical to a fulfilled married life.

This book is not intended to be a hammer but a tool that brings you closer together. You can't implement everything in this book without his agreement, support and even action. Thus, you need to let him read appropriate sections so the two of you are operating from the same knowledge base.

Savings

You may feel like the woman who asked us, "How can I save for retirement while putting my child through college?" We know it's tough to do both. The best answer may be company-sponsored retirement plans. While chapter 17 addresses most questions about where and when to invest, it doesn't cover those plans, so we'll say a little about them here.

Whether you work for a large or small company, employer-provided retirement plans can be a significant addition to your salary; they're often worth several thousand dollars in additional compensation per year. Surprisingly, however, few people even know whether their employers provide a pension plan, profit-sharing plan or 401-K plan into which they can make voluntary contributions. Employers will generally have a manual or brochure describing any retirement plans they make available. When you review those plans, you will almost invariably discover that such a plan is the first place you should make an investment for the long term.

Company-sponsored retirement plans come in many forms. They're commonly called thrift plans, profit-sharing plans, defined contribution plans, 401-K plans, money purchase plans or tax-sheltered annuity plans. They all allow the employee to contribute before-tax dollars, which will grow tax-deferred until retirement.

Contributing before-tax dollars means the amount of the contribution is subtracted from your income *before* any tax calculations are done. So as far as the IRS is concerned, you're paid less, which means you're also taxed less. And what you save in taxes makes up some or all of the amount you contribute to the plan. Thus, it's often possible to make regular contributions to such a plan without causing any decrease in your take-home pay.

After-tax dollars, on the other hand, are dollars from which the taxes have already been taken out. The value of contributing before-tax dollars, then, is that there's more money available to invest. For example, if you start with $1,000 to invest but you must first pay the taxes, you end up with only 70-80 percent ($700-$800) to invest. If you're investing before-tax dollars, however, you can contribute the entire $1,000.

Growing something tax-deferred means the taxes aren't payable on any income earned or appreciation in value until some later date. Monies contributed to retirement plans aren't taxed until the money is withdrawn. That allows for the compounding of a larger amount than would be possible if the taxes had to be paid every year.

The power of tax-deferred compounding can be dramatic. The following chart (fig. 8.1) illustrates three scenarios. One is a personal investment made after paying taxes on $5,000 of income. The second is a $5,000 contribution to a retirement plan in which the employer doesn't contribute anything. The third is a plan in which the employer contributes $0.50 for every dollar the employee contributes.

As you can easily see, not having taxes withheld from a salary can dramatically increase the amount available for investment. Although taxes must be paid upon withdrawal at retirement, the fund will usually have grown to a level that far exceeds what people would have accumulated on their own.

When the employer contributes to the plan, it's the same thing as earning an immediate return equal to the percentage contributed. In this illustration, a 50 percent contribution by the employer is equivalent to a 50 percent, no-risk return on your investment. If the plan grows in value, which it should, you can't help but be in a much better position by participating than you would be by investing on your own. This is true even if the plan has poor investment results. The mere facts of tax deferral and an employer contribution will dictate that participation in that type of plan should be your first investment choice.

Figure 8.1

What a $5,000 annual investment will
grow to assuming three tax environments

At End of Year	Taxable environment	Tax-deferred environment	Tax-deferred, with company matching 50%
5	22,282	33,578	50,367
10	53,827	87,656	131,484
15	98,485	174,749	262,123
20	161,708	315,012	472,519
25	251,214	540,909	811,363
30	377,927	904,717	1,357,076

Assumes 28% tax bracket and 10% investment growth.

Use of Debt

Later in this chapter we'll talk about student loans and home equity loans, and in other parts of the book we have talked about other kinds of debt. But here we want to talk about another decision that comes up generally during this season of life. That's the issue of whether or not to refinance your home.

People who purchased their homes ten to fifteen years ago and have seen them appreciate in value often consider refinancing in order to make use of that equity. If they purchased a home in the 1980s, they may have paid higher interest rates than those being offered today. Also, many people who have had adjustable-rate mortgages for some time find that their rate is now significantly higher than what a fixed-rate mortgage would cost. Refinancing then becomes a way to lower their monthly payments. This is especially attractive when you're considering the significant expenses of college for your kids.

Questions you should ask when considering refinancing a home are: (1) Is there a prepayment penalty on our existing mortgage? (2) What are the closing costs on the new mortgage: discount costs, title search fees, loan origination fees, appraisal fees, mortgage insurance premiums, attorney's fees and so on? (3) Will we live in the house long enough to recover those up-front refinancing costs? And can we control how long we'll be in our current home, or is it possible we'll be transferred? (4) Is there an alternative to refinancing that would also save significant interest costs over the life of the mortgage?

As a general rule, if you're going to live in your home for a minimum of two more years and the new interest rate is at least 2 percent lower than the old rate, it can make sense to refinance.

If you decide to refinance, consider a fifteen-year mortgage instead of the usual thirty-year deal. Your monthly payments will be somewhat higher, but you'll pay off the loan in half the time and save thousands of dollars in interest.

For example, on a fifteen-year, 10 percent mortgage of $75,000, the monthly payments are $806. The same mortgage on a thirty-year basis has monthly payments of $658. Assuming you paid both mortgages to maturity, the savings from the fifteen-year loan are $91,874. That's a huge sum of money saved by making slightly higher monthly payments. And if you've been in the house for a while, chances are your income has increased since the original mortgage was taken out, making the higher payments on the fifteen-year mortgage affordable.

A good alternative to refinancing your home is to double up on your monthly mortgage payments. In many cases you can pay the home off in five or six years rather than thirty. A less-expensive choice is to pay an additional $25 to $50 per month toward the principal and thereby reduce the mortgage period by several years, saving a bundle in interest. Your lender should be able to show you the effects of increasing your payments.

Whether you're refinancing your existing home or buying a new house, it's wise to shop, shop, shop for a mortgage. Check the mortgage companies, banks, and savings and loans thoroughly, as they change their rates and terms weekly. Because of the magic of compounding, it's worth considerable dollars to save as little as a quarter of a percent on your mortgage rate. Closing costs can also be very different from lender to lender.

What you should *not* do in refinancing your home is to take out a bigger mortgage and consume the excess without a plan for using it. To spend it on vacations or consumable items destroys what is probably your most-significant asset, your equity in your home.

Insurance

In terms of total dollars of life and disability insurance coverage, this is probably your season of greatest need. Your living expenses are at their highest level; mortgage balances are typically at their highest level; college costs are just around the corner; transportation and car costs are at their highest level. Therefore, the need to provide for the loss of income from the family breadwinners is also at its highest level. You should never be underinsured, especially with the relatively low cost of life insurance today, but absolutely not now.

It's also time to make sure your wills are still consistent with your plans, economic circumstances and desires. You and your attorney should review them if two years have passed since the last review.

Paying for College Education

College can cost anywhere from $2,000 to $30,000 a year and is escalating at the rate of about 7 percent per year. Yet very few parents have adequately prepared to pay for their children's college education. Consequently, they have a big problem when their kids reach that age. Assuming there are no rich grandparents or financial windfalls, there are really only five sources of college money:

1. The parents' current income.
2. Scholarships or grants.
3. Income generated by the student.
4. The sale of assets by the parents.
5. College loans or other debt.

Scholarships and grants are an ideal way to pay for college, as that means the student has qualified for them in some way. They can't be planned on, however, and there obviously aren't enough for every student (or even most).

Having the money saved ahead of time is the surest way to pay for college. But if that hasn't happened and no scholarship or grant money is available to your child, you'll need to use one or more of the other three methods.

Most parents plan to use their current income as a significant portion of the funds for college. That means they're planning to decrease their expenses, or else they've been saving some excess funds out of a positive cash flow. Lastly, they may be expecting their income to go up to create a positive cash flow.

Paying for college out of current income is so difficult because you're using only after-tax dollars. For example, if the college bill is $10,000 per year, the par-

You should never be underinsured, but absolutely not now.

ents must earn approximately $20,000 in order to pay the taxes and tithe and still have $10,000 left for college expenses. If the four-year total costs are $40,000, somehow the parents must earn $80,000 above and beyond their other needs.

Obviously, even those who have large incomes will see a high percentage of their income going toward college education. If more than one child at a time is in college, the financial burden multiplies. Since college costs are nondeductible, there's not even a tax benefit to paying them.

One alternative, which is actually very positive, is for students to work to help defray the costs. This is not done nearly as much anymore as was customary in our day, when our parents were coming out of the Depression and a college education was still a luxury.

Choosing to have your children work to provide some of their college expenses may mean they take longer to get through school than the traditional four years. That certainly is no great sacrifice for them. The biggest advantage is that they'll have a greater appreciation for a college education if they help pay for it.

Another financing possibility is the sale of assets. Those could be either investment assets or personal assets. A personal asset is something purchased for personal use, such as a boat or car. An investment asset has generally been bought with the idea that it will increase in value and be used to meet a long-term goal. Kids' college education obviously may be one such goal.

You may have assets in retirement plans such as IRAs that could be used for college education. The advantage of using such funds is that you avoid going into debt to pay for college. However, interest or tax penalties may be associated with the sale of those assets.

You need to determine whether the costs of borrowing are more or less than the costs associated with using an investment or retirement asset. A financial professional can help you decide that. Our first inclination would always be to sell assets as opposed to taking on debt, but many factors need to be considered, and it's never a simple, clear-cut decision.

If borrowing seems to make sense to pay for your kids' education, you have three primary sources to consider. They are the cash surrender value from whole-life insurance policies, a home equity loan and student loans.

Borrowing from life insurance policies is usually the best of those alternatives. Money borrowed from whole-life policies is called a life insurance loan, but it's not really debt. You have accumulated those funds in the life insurance product, and they're yours any time you choose to cancel the policy.

Thus, when you borrow from your life insurance, you're effectively borrowing from yourself. You also have a guaranteed way to repay the loan: When you die (a guaranteed event), the amount borrowed is paid from the proceeds of the policy. (In other words, your beneficiaries get paid that much less than they would have otherwise.) The interest rate is specified in the insurance contract.

That rate can be very low for older policies but is fairly high and variable for newer policies. The interest is not tax deductible, but this is still a good source of borrowing that should be considered.

Should you even bother to repay life insurance loans? It's not required, since the company can just deduct the outstanding balance from the amount it pays to your beneficiaries. The answer depends on the company itself. If it's a quality company with a history of increasing dividends (which are really returns of excess premiums) to policy holders, repaying the loan makes sense. It will reduce your interest costs each year and also allow for a tax-free cash value buildup within the policy. In other words, it can be an excellent investment.

A second source of borrowing would be the home equity loan. The interest charged on such a loan will typically be tax deductible. Like any form of debt, however, it may be a lot easier to get than it is to pay off. Additionally, a home equity loan puts your home at risk. One other caution is that the interest rate may have no ceiling to it; therefore, your interest costs may end up being much higher than you anticipated. For all these reasons, using a home equity loan to pay for college is not as much a financial question as it is a priority question. That is, the risks involved make this a far-from-ideal way to pay for college, and you have to decide if being able to cover those costs is worth the risks.

Student loans can also be used to fund college education. They may be the only way some young people can pay for college. Since a college degree typically improves their economic possibilities by making them eligible for higher-paying jobs, student loans may make good economic sense.

The danger, however, is that there's no guaranteed way to repay the loan. Certain types of after-college work don't pay well enough to make timely repayment possible. If students know they'll be taking such positions, they should never incur a student loan lest they not be able to enter the career God has called them to. The better alternative would be to stretch out their college education over several years and work their way through school.

Before borrowing money from any source for a college education, the question needs to be asked, "Are there any other alternatives?" The second question to ask is "Am I denying God an opportunity to provide the necessary funds by taking on this debt?"

Conclusion

We've all heard the saying "He slept like a baby." Babies enjoy a peace and tranquility that many of us no longer experience. A host of things—college education, a changing relationship with your husband, career changes, huge debt loads—can cause you to be anxious. Babies, on the other hand, are motivated by just a few basic needs. And once those needs are met, they have little to concern themselves with, so they can rest in total peace.

In our minds, true financial freedom comes when money and financial decisions do not dominate the thought life. In other words, you're financially free when you're free from worry caused by any possible use or misuse of money. Therefore, you can sleep like a baby.

The most common belief about financial freedom is that if you have enough money, you'll ultimately be free. That money is expected to come from pay raises, increases in investment values, business successes or something that gives you enough wealth to be entirely self-sufficient. Most believe we can reach some point where the day-to-day concerns about money will no longer worry us, and therefore we'll be free.

The truth, however, is that no amount of money will ever provide financial freedom. In fact, just the opposite may be the case: The more money you have, the more alternatives you have for spending it, which may change your priorities. Howard Hughes was one of the world's wealthiest men at the time of his death, yet he lived in fear and anxiety for the last many years of his life. He was fabulously wealthy, but he was not free.

To be truly free from the love of money as well as from money worries, four things are required. First, you must have a proper belief system regarding money (covered in chap. 2). Second, you need a money management system that works for your family. Third, you need a decision-making process so that when you make financial choices, you can be sure you've considered all the objectives and all the alternatives. Fourth and most important, the ultimate key to financial freedom is giving back to God the resources He has entrusted to you. This chapter has outlined some significant challenges common to this period of life, but God is able to meet our needs and has promised to do so.

CHAPTER NINE

The Empty Nest

*L*ike many daughters of aging parents, Sandy Berman didn't recognize at first how far her mother and father had slipped. 'You are so used to your parents' being mentally competent that you don't realize what you're dealing with for a long time,' says the Northridge, Calif., schoolteacher, 47. Her parents had been living with trash piling up in their home for almost a year when Berman finally convinced them to move closer. But the move only hastened their decline. Berman's father, 83, became forgetful and overdosed on his insulin. Her mother, 74, couldn't find her way from the bedroom to the bathroom. For months, Berman called every morning before going to work, and stopped by every afternoon. 'I was going to make everything right, and better and perfect,' she says. 'But everything I did turned into mush.'"

So begins a *Newsweek* article ("Trading Places," 7-16-90, p. 48) describing how more and more women are struggling to care for their aging parents while still juggling all their other responsibilities. It's a challenge common to the empty-nest time of life, and potentially one of the most frustrating. We'll deal with it in detail later in this chapter.

The empty nest can be a difficult transition time in anyone's life. The responsibility of providing for your children and passing a value system on to them has been accomplished. Now, as you look toward the future, what you see is retirement, widowhood, grandparenting, meeting significant financial needs of your children and perhaps the care of aging parents. Talk about going from the frying pan into the fire!

Since you're done raising and educating children, your home mortgage may be close to being paid off, retirement plans may have been growing in value, and perhaps even some investments have been growing in value, you may well have more money available than you ever dreamed possible. The demand for those resources, however, can be significant. In addition to the uncertainties mentioned above, you may have deferred many desires until now—for example, increased giving, paying off the home mortgage and doing more effective tax planning.

The two primary planning needs are to put together a long-range plan integrating those desires and opportunities and to have an estate plan that reflects your wishes and unique needs. The main financial fear women face at this season of life is not being able to live as well in the future as they are today.

That's a legitimate concern, and we're going to address it in this chapter along with some other common questions and concerns. We'll have sections discussing increased giving, paying off your home mortgage, planning for retirement, estate planning, whether or not to move to a smaller house, creating expectations in grown children, tax planning and caring for aging parents.

Increased Giving

If in fact you find yourself with an increased ability to give now, just how much should you give? There are three different giving levels to consider.

The first level is *proportionate giving:* "On the first day of every week, each one of you should set aside a sum of money in keeping with his income, saving it up, so that when I come no collections will have to be made" (1 Cor. 16:2). We're to give as God has prospered us. Though an argument can be made for the tithe's being 10 percent of one's income, nowhere in the New Testament is a percentage given or implied. So giving isn't limited to 10 percent. It's only limited by how much God has prospered you, which may mean you have the privilege and blessing of giving well beyond the tithe.

The second level is *planned giving.* One of the primary reasons for a long-range financial plan is to integrate the conflicting needs and uses of money, such as giving versus debt payoff. When you do a financial plan, you're predetermining how much and where to give. And planned giving is simply deciding to give up something in order to give—a vacation, a life-style desire or a savings account, for example. We call this the "could give" level, and you do this not because you expect a material blessing but rather a spiritual one.

When people plan to give, they often give far beyond what they thought possible. In many cases, it's as much as five to ten times more than they were giving.

The third level of giving is *precommitted giving.* If your income goes up or your expenses decrease unexpectedly, the new cash surplus could be precommitted to giving. If you don't make such a precommitment to giving all or a portion of unexpected surpluses, the chances are very good you won't give. A wealthy businessman once told Ron, "There's not a businessman worth his salt who doesn't have use for a spare million." We always have ways to spend unexpected dollars. So make a precommitment to give away part or all of your unexpected surpluses. Some would call this a faith gift.

A faith gift is at a level above proportionate and planned giving because in both of the first two cases, you can "see" where the resources are that the giving is going to come from. Precommitted giving, on the other hand, is giving out of resources you don't now see but that God, in His wisdom and grace, may choose to bless you with.

We're reminded of what Jim Elliot, the martyred missionary, said: "He is no fool who gives what he cannot keep to gain what he cannot lose." He wasn't speaking directly to the issue of charitable giving, but the principle certainly applies.

How Tax Law Affects Your Giving

The United States is one of the few countries that allows charitable deductions from income before computing income taxes. Because it's one of the surest ways to get a tax break, many people use charitable giving as a significant tax-planning tool.

Such giving should *never* be done just to get a tax deduction. However, wisdom would say that when you do give charitably, you should take full advantage of the law. That *doesn't* mean all giving should be deductible giving. If the only motive for giving is a tax deduction, we question whether there's any spiritual

---

*G*iving is one of the ways God chooses to meet the needs of His people. Some have and should give; others don't have and need to receive.

---

benefit to it. We should give out of obedience to God's Word. Giving is one of the ways God chooses to meet the needs of His people. Some have and should give; others don't have and need to receive.

With that said, you should be aware of certain types of giving and techniques and use them if they fit your situation.

Gifts of Cash

Gifts of cash to a church, hospital, parachurch ministry, mission organization or other not-for-profit organization are fully deductible up to 50 percent of your adjusted gross income. The amounts that are not deductible in the year of the gift because of going over 50 percent of your income can be used in subsequent years as deductions against future years' income. Cash is rarely questioned as a charitable deduction.

When cash less than 50 percent of your adjusted gross income is given, you enjoy a tax savings of some amount, depending on your tax bracket. If you're in the 25 percent bracket and you give $1,000, the government allows you to deduct the $1,000 from your income, thereby reducing your taxes by 25 percent of the $1,000, or $250. The net cost to you is then the difference between $1,000 and $250, or $750. So it costs you only $750 to give $1,000.

Some people do substantial charitable giving near the end of the year to get a tax break for that year. For example, they may do all the next year's giving in the current year. That requires planning and is certainly legal, but remember that the motive for charitable giving should never be a tax deduction. However, if you can use the strategy to your advantage, the law encourages you to do so, and it's not unethical.

Gifts of Appreciated Property

If you give a piece of property (such as stocks or real estate) that has appreciated in value since you bought it, you can deduct the full fair market value of the property. For example, if you purchased stock for $10,000 more than twelve months ago and it has appreciated in value to $20,000, you're allowed to deduct the entire $20,000. If you're in the 25 percent tax bracket, your tax savings will be 25 percent of the $20,000, or $5,000.

Upon receipt of the stock certificates, the charity can sell them and have $20,000 to use as it sees fit. If you had *sold* the stock and contributed the proceeds of the sale rather than giving the certificates themselves, you first would have paid $2,500 in taxes (the $10,000 gain times 25%), leaving only $17,500 in cash to give to the charity.

By receiving the stock certificates directly, the charity benefits by $2,500, and you benefit by even more: You get a bigger tax deduction, and you avoid paying tax on the sale of the appreciated property. It's possible, however, that by making such a gift, you could subject yourself to a special tax called the alternative minimum tax. This is a complex enough area that you should check with an accountant, an attorney or the charity before making the gift.

Establishing a Charitable Trust

In addition to making outright gifts of cash or appreciated property, some people set up one of two types of charitable trusts. Each of these sophisticated trusts has many variations, so our only purpose here is to bring them to your attention. If you think you might want to use them, once again you should seek expert help.

A *charitable remainder trust* enables you to give assets to a charity, receiving a deduction in the year they're contributed while at the same time allowing you or members of your family to receive all the income the property generates. After a specified time period, the trust terminates and the charity receives outright ownership of the property.

A *charitable lead trust* works in the opposite way. The income generated by the property during the term of the trust goes to the charity, but the property reverts to you or your family at some point in the future. A current income deduction is not allowed for the gift to the trust (as is the case with the charitable remainder trust). However, what you have done is to shift income that would have been taxed to a charity for its use.

Through the use of creative charitable techniques in estate planning, sale of a business, income shifting to family members and so on, it's possible to reduce income taxes, save estate taxes and use those savings to benefit a charity to a much greater extent than would be the case otherwise. Only rarely will creative planning not benefit both the individual donor and the recipient charity.

Paying Off the Home Mortgage

Close your eyes for a minute and imagine what it would it would be like to have no debt at all, including no mortgage on your home. Chances are, it gave you a feeling of security. And that raises the question, Why do so many people who could be totally out of debt remain in debt? A recent headline in the Atlanta newspaper read, "Don't Use Windfall to Pay Off Mortgage." There's a perception that debt is wise for two reasons: first, the interest paid on borrowed money is tax deductible, thereby reducing your tax liability; second, keeping the money invested that could be used to pay off debt is generally touted as the wise thing to do.

In previous chapters, we've emphasized that paying off credit card and installment debt is the same thing as making an 18 to 21 percent investment. Well, the same holds true for paying off a mortgage. If you have a $50,000, 10 percent mortgage and a $50,000 investment, not using the investment to pay off the mortgage implies you can earn 10 percent *risk-free* with that investment. Why?

Paying off the mortgage with the $50,000 is a *guaranteed* way to effectively increase your cash flow and earnings by 10 percent of the $50,000. You no longer have the mortgage payment, and therefore you'll save annually both the payment on the principal plus $5,000 you would have been paying in interest. It's true that the interest paid on a mortgage is tax deductible, but the tax break is offset by not having the interest expense in the first place and being able to *earn* interest by investing that savings.

The question is whether you can earn more than 10 percent *risk-free* with your investments. Experience shows that it's extremely difficult to earn more consistently than you're paying in mortgage interest. Granted, you may have a very low mortgage rate, and in that case you may be able to earn more than you're paying. But we assure you, you're *not* earning more *risk-free*.

Note, however, that you should not use *all* your savings to pay off your mortgage. You should always keep an emergency fund as described in the sequential investment strategy (see chap. 17).

An alternative to paying off your mortgage in a lump sum is to make prepayments of principal. Perhaps every year you can make one extra payment or even a larger lump sum payment. Your monthly payments may not go down as a result, but the mortgage will be paid off in significantly less time. If you have a thirty-year mortgage at 10 percent and make one extra payment per year, for example, you'll pay off the loan in just twenty-one years.

If making prepayments does not lower your monthly payments, realize that if you miss a payment in the future, you still could be in default on your mortgage, even though you had paid ahead significantly. Some lenders, however, *will* consider your prepayments as advance payments, and in that case you would not be in default if you missed a payment. To determine which type of mortgage you have, talk to your lender.

Paying off your mortgage early not only makes good sense emotionally and psychologically, but also from an investment standpoint. It gives you a decent *risk-free* return, along with the peace of mind.

Planning for Retirement

Planning for retirement is the subject of the entire next chapter. However, it almost goes without saying that you should be preparing for it already. And the two key questions you need to answer are these: How much will I need at retirement to live the rest of my life, and how do I accumulate enough?

Two main variables will greatly influence the answers. First is the life-style you desire to provide for, and second is the time you have until retirement. Obviously, the lower the life-style and the greater the amount of time, the easier it will be to provide for retirement. Conversely, the shorter the time and the higher the life-style, the more difficult it will be. Concern about being able to live as well in the future as you are today is what drives consideration of this topic.

Besides reading the next chapter, you'll also benefit from reading chapter 17 on how to invest and rereading chapters 2 and 3 (the cornerstones of financial success).

Estate Planning

One of the certainties of life is that it will end. Yet many normally prudent people ignore that reality in their planning. The death of either spouse will basically throw out the window the planning that's been done up to that point. Goals change, as do circumstances. The worst mistake is to not face the reality of death and plan for it.

Like estate planning, this is an area that calls for your immediate, careful attention. It's also an area you need to discuss thoroughly with your husband, and you need to talk it through at least once a year, as circumstances change constantly. Rather than repeat our detailed treatment of estate planning in every chapter, we ask you to please turn to that section in the life insurance chapter (chap. 15). You would also benefit from reading the sections on wills in chapters 6 and 7.

Smaller Home

At this time of life, you begin to think about downsizing your home. There are many emotional and practical aspects to that decision, and tax consequences need to be considered as well. However, the tax considerations should be only one part of your decision making, not necessarily the driving force.

An older couple had five adult children who grew up in a large home on several acres of land. Now that the children were gone, the home seemed even bigger than it was before, and the couple wondered if they should continue to spend so much to keep up a large house. Ron had been asked to evaluate the sale of the home from a financial standpoint. As they discussed the possible sale, it became clear that the home represented something the parents didn't want to lose: The grandkids really looked forward to a vacation each summer at Grandma and Grandpa's home.

As the couple discussed the issue in that light, they decided they were willing to continue spending the extra money. Their home offered tradition, stability and opportunities to build once-in-a-lifetime memories. We were deeply affected by our conversation with them, deciding that we, too, would like to hold on to the home where our children grew up and to which they can always come back.

By the time most couples reach their fifties, they live in homes that have appreciated greatly in value. It may very well be that your first home cost $20,000, and you're now living in a home with a value of $200,000. The gain of $180,000 represents the profit coming from inflation. When that home is sold, there will be a tax on the gain.

That tax is mitigated, however, by a one-time exemption on $125,000 of gain for taxpayers over fifty-five. For example, if you're sixty years old, sell your

There's nothing bad about having to pay taxes when you've made a large profit.

home for $200,000 and it originally cost you $20,000, only $55,000 of the gain will be taxable. The exemption is on the sale of the home and not per taxpayer. In other words, a couple doesn't get $250,000 of exemptions; rather, it's a $125,000 exemption for the couple together.

If you purchase a smaller home, only *a portion* of the gain from the sale of your first home will be taxable. The part you reinvest in another home is not taxed until you ultimately sell your home and do not buy another.

Here again, your decisions should not be driven by the tax consequences: they merely need to be considered and planned for. There's nothing bad about having to pay taxes when you've made a large profit. It's true the profit may be due to inflation rather than a real increase in the value of the home, but inflation also means you'll be paying the taxes with cheaper dollars.

Creating Expectations in Grown Children

Because this is a time when perhaps you have sold your home and have greater cash flows and lesser financial needs, your children may expect financial help that you may or may not want to give. Even as you're probably becoming more financially free, they're hitting the stage of life with young children and significant needs. Buying homes, paying off student debt and financial problems may create pressures on your kids that you can well appreciate because you've been there yourself.

The primary challenge is to communicate to your children, *before* they have a need, what is reasonable to expect from you in the way of assistance. It's not a question of what's right and wrong but rather giving them proper expectations so they don't experience what we earlier called a coping gap.

We personally think it's a privilege to help our kids with significant financial needs. Many of us would like to do so since we ourselves didn't have that kind of help. We probably didn't suffer as a consequence, but life would have been easier if we had received the help we're now able to give our children.

In providing such help, you have to ask yourself some tough questions: (1) Are you contributing to a life-style they'll have a hard time maintaining in the future? (2) Are you contributing to a life-style you don't want them to have? (3) Are you exercising undue control over them through your financial help?

We believe you should *give* children money as opposed to loaning it to them. The Bible says, "The borrower becomes the lender's slave." When you loan your kids money, even with the best of intentions, you've created a debtor-lender relationship that's fraught with potential problems.

If you do decide to make your kids a loan because you can't afford to give them the money, the amount should be documented in writing, along with a stated repayment period and a defined interest rate. That way, both of you have the same expectations on repayment, and you avoid later problems caused by differing intentions.

In helping your children financially, be careful that you're not denying God an opportunity to work in their lives and that you're not compounding problems for them later. Make sure your intentions and reasons are well communicated so you're not creating improper expectations for them. The best time to start that communication is when they're younger, even before they go on to college, so you don't give them time to create improper expectations in their own minds.

Remember that you're a steward of God's resources, and He has called you to provide for your family, not protect them from His dealings with them. Only God in His sovereignty and grace can literally protect any of us. We can provide for our families, but we can't perform the role of God in their lives.

Tax Planning

With an increased positive cash flow, you may have more opportunities to reduce your taxes. Remember, however, that the only ways to reduce taxes are to either reduce income or increase expenses. Both have a negative impact on your cash flow, but both do reduce your taxes.

The two primary ways to reduce taxes at this time are to increase your charitable giving or increase your contributions to retirement plans.

Increased contributions to retirement plans can be through either company-sponsored or self-funding plans. Many kinds of plans are available, including IRAs, Keoghs, SEPs, 401-Ks, qualified pension plans, profit-sharing plans, 403-B plans and maybe even some others. Contributions to retirement plans take away cash flow and may reduce income, but they also reduce taxes and build savings for retirement.

Our general recommendation is to put as much away toward retirement as is consistent with your needs and goals. You'll need to balance the desires to pay off debt, increase charitable giving, help children, save for retirement and reduce taxes. Every one of us deals with limited resources, so decisions about balancing conflicting goals and priorities are difficult and probably ever changing. What was right this year may not be right next year. Remember, however, that there's not one right answer. Rather, we have to prioritize how we're going to use excess income.

Caring for Aging Parents

In the May 1989 issue of our firm's newsletter, Steve Franklin from our staff contributed an article titled "Planning for Your Parents." That article summarizes well the issues relative to caring for aging parents, and much of what follows originated in Steve's article.

Few Christians plan for the time when their parents can no longer care for themselves either physically or financially. Let's face it: It's awkward, maybe a bit embarrassing and difficult to even know how to approach the subject with those who have raised you. It's almost like meddling in business that's not yours. You hope it will go away or take care of itself. But you know down deep that it won't, and eventually you'll be faced with some tough decisions if your parents live long enough.

Many of us must either put our parents (one or both) in some sort of extended-care facility or have them live with us until they die. Depending on how they've managed their finances, we'll be faced with assisting them in making prudent expenditures for their aging care or financially helping them.

First Timothy 5:8 provides clear instruction regarding our responsibility to care for family members: "If anyone does not provide for his relatives, and especially for his immediate family, he has denied the faith and is worse than an unbeliever." James 1:27 adds this insight: "Religion that God our Father accepts as pure and faultless is this: to look after all orphans and widows in their distress and to keep oneself from being polluted by the world."

Those verses can serve as a basis for sitting down right now with your parents, expressing your desire to fulfill your responsibility prudently, and beginning to develop a game plan for a practical decision in the future. If one of your parents is already deceased, it should intensify your motivation to begin this process as soon as possible.

The two basic subjects you need to discuss with your parents are where to live, particularly after one parent has died, and the financial aspects of long-term care.

Where to Live

The decision either to put your parents into a nursing home or have them come live with you is loaded with emotion, anxiety and a myriad of concerns. There are some practical advantages to having your parents live in a professional, well-run nursing home or extended-care facility: (1) socialization with people of their own age and similar interests; (2) care by trained professionals; and (3) scheduled freedom for you and your family.

However, extended-care facilities are expensive. Many people also experience a great amount of guilt by putting their parents in a "home." Finally, you lose the opportunities for your children to develop intimate relationships with their grandparents.

Although the Bible doesn't specifically command that we have our aging parents live with us, the spirit of 1 Timothy 5:8 and James 1:27 suggests we give serious consideration to the idea, understanding that empathy and patience will have to be exercised regularly. The benefits to your family can include these:

1. Opportunity for shared wisdom. Parents have a wealth of wisdom to share with us if we'll take the time to ask about their life experiences, beliefs, fears, joys and so on—and if we'll take the time to listen.

2. Opportunity for bonding. The only way deep, rich family bonds are developed is by frequently spending time together and communicating. Our mobile society has virtually destroyed the extended-family relationships God intended for us. Elderly parents can be true blessings to us and our children.

3. Opportunity for service. There's no more worthy Christian service than caring for your parents, particularly if they're physically ill and require a great deal

There's no more worthy Christian service than caring for your parents.

of attention and sacrifice. This builds the kind of character and servant spirit Christ exhorted His disciples to have.

4. Opportunity for love. No one can love and care for your parents like you. Caring for aging parents is perhaps the greatest opportunity God gives us to express our love for them in the truest sense of the word.

Financial Considerations

In a *U.S. News & World Report* article titled "Paying for Long-Term Care" (Jan. 23, 1989), the writer noted that most insurance policies do not adequately cover the cost of prolonged nursing home stays or home care: "Without substantial assets or some sort of supplemental insurance, many people in need of such care could be forced to turn to their children for help or to Medicaid, the government welfare program for the poor." Whether you and your parents decide they will live in an extended-care facility or at home, financial considerations must be a candid part of your discussion.

Long-term care (LTC) insurance makes sense only for people with incomes over $15,000 a year and assets over $30,000 at retirement (excluding your home). These policies vary widely in coverage, so you must do your homework when considering them. A helpful booklet is "The Consumers Guide to Long-Term Care Insurance" from the Health Insurance Association of America, P.O. Box 41455, Washington, D.C. 20018.

Having parents come live with you involves other financial considerations as well. Your home may require an addition; transportation must be considered; and myriad other subjects should be discussed. The key is to openly, frankly and genuinely express concern for your parent's welfare. Now is the time to begin planning for the spiritual responsibility God has entrusted to you.

Conclusion

We began this chapter by saying the empty-nest season is often a time of major financial opportunity. Significant financial obligations have been met and income is going up, so your cash flow has probably never been better. But those who think that having more money makes life easier have never had more money. More money creates more opportunities and many more decisions to make, complicating life considerably. That's probably one reason our Lord challenged those who have a great deal to never let financial resources, opportunities, problems and decisions become the focus of their lives. "It is easier for a camel to go through the eye of a needle," He said, "than for a rich man to enter into the kingdom of God" (Matt. 19:24).

We hope this chapter has helped to answer some of the common questions of this season and so make your life somewhat more orderly. But having more will not make life any easier emotionally and spiritually.

CHAPTER TEN

Retirement: Work's End or Second Wind?

*I*f you ever take a vacation to Florida during the winter, you may experience a lot of frustration. Finding a place to eat dinner is difficult; every restaurant seems to be packed from 5:00 P.M. until 8:00 P.M. Driving is virtually impossible, especially near the beaches, because the roads are so crowded. Trying to play golf or visit Disney World may also be impossible because of the multitudes. And if you look at the people, you see that most appear to be retirement age.

The word *retirement* conjures up all sorts of images. According to the dictionary, retirement is "withdrawal from one's position or occupation or from active working life." Retirement could mean ceasing to work altogether, or it could simply mean a change in vocation.

Only in North America is it possible for large numbers of people (but not everyone) to quit working at some age. Pension plans funded by companies, unions and other groups, as well as Social Security and the general affluence of Americans, have made retirement a viable option to a majority of people. In the rest of the world, quitting work is generally not an option. And if you reflect on the Bible, it's hard to think of anyone who literally retired in those days.

The real question, however, is probably not *can* you retire, but rather *should* you quit working? We'll consider both questions here. Again, not everyone will be able to retire, but let's assume for the moment that you can afford to do so and ask, What does retirement mean?

To help answer this question, let's look at Luke 12:16-21: "And he told them this parable: 'The ground of a certain rich man produced a good crop. He thought to himself, "What shall I do? I have no place to store my crops." Then he said, "This is what I'll do. I will tear down my barns and build bigger ones, and there I will store all my grain and my goods. And I'll say to myself, 'You have plenty of good things laid up for many years. Take life easy; eat, drink and be merry.'" But God said to him, "You fool! This very night your life will be demanded from you. Then who will get what you have prepared for yourself?" This is how it will be with anyone who stores up things for himself but is not rich toward God.'"

The man in that parable intended to take life easy, to eat, drink and be merry. But God said to him, "You fool." We Christians are not called to a life of eating, drinking and making merry. Instead, God has called us to a life of purpose and accomplishment for the cause of Christ. We're here on earth as pilgrims for a brief time. During that time, all our energies and activities should be directed toward accomplishing God's purposes for us.

Therefore, we may retire from a particular occupation, but it shouldn't be to live a life of ease. Rather, it should be because God has called us to another activity, ministry or vocation. Ron likes to tell people he retired at age thirty-five, which he did from the business he had started several years before. In reality, of course, he just changed vocations.

Many people become confused by equating financial independence with retirement. They're not the same thing. Many people are financially independent but far from retired. A good friend recently sold his business to devote full time to a ministry to business people. He's now so busy ministering that he has little time to manage the wealth God has entrusted to him.

We must answer a basic question of life: Why am I here? At some point, all of us will stand before our Lord and give an account of how we've used our time (see 2 Cor. 5:10). We certainly don't want to have to say that in our last fifteen years, all we accomplished was to read one novel a week, lower our golf handicap ten strokes or try thirty-seven different restaurants offering a senior citizens' discount. None of those activities is bad in itself, but such pursuits *are* wrong if they become the overriding motivation in a person's life.

One of the greatest resources available to the Christian community is older saints who have so much wisdom and knowledge to offer. Regardless of our age, our mindset should be that, in light of eternity, we have so little time and so much to do. Consider Moses, who didn't even begin his work for the cause of God until age eighty. In Psalm 90:12 he prayed, "Teach us to number our days aright, that we may gain a heart of wisdom."

Those who do quit income-producing work face this large and obvious question: How much money do I need to last the rest of my life? Health care and retire-

*R*egardless of our age, our mindset should be that, in light of eternity, we have so little time and so much to do.

ment income are probably the two biggest issues. The survey conducted for this book indicated that as women reach retirement age, they're very concerned about whether they'll be able to live as well in the future as they can today.

This chapter addresses common questions about the retirement years. Those questions are: Will you have enough resources to live the rest of your life? How should you take pension benefits from your employer? When should you take Social Security benefits, and will Social Security last? How do you preserve investments in uncertain economic times? And should you continue a life insurance program?

How Much Is Enough?

Money magazine ran an article on retirement in 1989 that included the chart we have reproduced here as figure 10.1. While not guaranteeing accuracy on every number, this chart will give you a good yardstick for determining what you need to do between now and retirement to have enough when the time comes.

Specifically, this worksheet will help you estimate how much you must save each year for retirement. It assumes your investments will earn 3 percent after inflation, about the historical average for a conservative portfolio of stocks, bonds and cash. For extra safety, the worksheet also assumes you will live ten years beyond the life expectancy of a sixty-five-year-old in 1989. All amounts are in today's dollars. If you're less than ten years from leaving work, update your calculation annually. If retirement is further off, do so every two years.

Figure 10.1

RUNNING THE NUMBERS ON RETIREMENT

1 Annual income needed in retirement $40,000 in current dollars
(rough estimate 70% of current income)

2 Expected Social Security benefit $10,788 in current dollars
(for exact figure, call Social Security Admin. 800-234-5772;
      rough estimate $10,788 if you make more than $48,000
            $ 9,300 if you make $25,000)

3 Expected company pension benefit $ 0 in current dollars
(for exact figure, call benefits counselor at work;
   rough estimate 1.5% x current salary x
           multiply years of service at retirement)

4 Expected income from retirement benefits $10,788 in current dollars
(line 2 plus line 3)

5 Annual retirement income needed from savings $29,212 in current dollars
(line 1 minus line 4)

**6 Amount you must save by retirement in
today's dollars**
(line 5 times multiplier from table A)   Retirement age   60
                        Multiplier   21.0 $613,452 in current dollars

7 Amount you have saved already:
IRAs and KEOGHS $50,000
Employer savings (401-Ks, ESOPs, etc.)   ——
Other investments (CDs, stocks, etc.) $30,000
Optional (portion of current home equity) $50,000 $130,000 in current dollars

8 Value of your retirement savings at retirement
(line 7 times multiplier from table B)   Current age   38
                        Yrs to retirement 22
                        Multiplier   1.81 $235,300 in future dollars

9 Amount of retirement capital still needed $378,152
(line 6 minus line 8)

10 Total annual savings still needed
(line 9 times multiplier from table C)   Multiplier   0.037 $13,992

**11 Annual employer contributions to company
savings plans** $ 0
(401-Ks, ESOPs, SEPs, profit-sharing plans)

**12 Annual amount you need to set aside in
today's dollars** $13,992
(line 10 minus line 11)

Table A		Table B		Table C	
Retirement Age	Multiplier	Years until retirement	Multiplier	Years until retirement	Multiplier
55	22.8	1	1.03	1	1.000
56	22.5	3	1.09	3	0.324
57	22.1	5	1.16	5	0.188
58	21.8	7	1.23	7	0.131
59	21.4	9	1.30	9	0.098
60	21.0	11	1.38	11	0.078
61	20.6	13	1.47	13	0.064
62	20.2	15	1.56	15	0.054
63	19.8	20	1.81	20	0.037
64	19.3	25	2.09	25	0.027
65	18.9	30	2.43	30	0.021
66	18.4				
67	17.9				

From *MONEY Guide 1989*, p. 29. Reprinted from *MONEY* magazine by special permission; copyright 1989 The Time Inc. Magazine Company.

Line 1 calls for the annual income needed in retirement. A rule of thumb is that 70 percent of your current income will be needed to maintain your present standard of living. It's not 100 percent because some of your income will be from nontaxable sources, and many of your expenses will be going down over time (e.g., a mortgage payment).

To get a more accurate number for your retirement needs, use the budget worksheets at the end of chapter 4. Envision yourself living in retirement, and think through what expenses you'll continue to have. What would you like your life to be like in that season?

Line 2 is expected Social Security benefits, which may or may not be applicable to your situation. Line 3 also may or may not be applicable, depending on where you're employed; it's the expected pension benefit, exclusive of personal pensions such as IRAs and Keogh plans. Line 4 is the total of lines 2 and 3. Line 5 is the difference between lines 1 and 4.

Line 6 is a calculation of the amount you must have on hand by retirement in today's dollars, taking into account both your life expectancy and inflation. We used this chart because the mathematics have already been done for those variables.

Line 7 is a calculation of the amount you've already accumulated toward retirement. Line 8 is all the savings you have now, compounded until retirement. Line 9 is the difference between lines 7 and 6, or the amount you still need to accumulate. Line 10 is a calculation of the *annual* savings still needed. Line 11 is the amount that's now being contributed toward retirement by you or your employer. Line 12 is the difference between lines 10 and 11 and is the amount you'll need to save out of personal cash flow between now and retirement.

This chart assumes neither you nor your husband will continue to work after retirement age. It also doesn't consider major financial needs (e.g., caring for aging parents), inheritances you could receive or other dramatic changes in your economic situation. It will give you a good place to start, however, in seeing whether you're even close to providing for retirement. You can never accumulate enough to be financially secure, as we pointed out in chapter 1; only God provides ultimate security. But the Christian's part is to plan with prudence.

Figure 10.2 depicts what $100,000 will be worth at the end of varying time periods assuming different inflation rates. It shows, for example, that $100,000 today will be worth $37,689 at the end of twenty years with an annual inflation rate of 5 percent. To put it another way, figure 10.3 depicts how much you would need to buy what $100,000 will buy today. At a 5 percent inflation rate, at the end of twenty years you would need $265,330.

Figure 10.2
What $100,000 will be worth in the future assuming various inflation rates

At End of Year	Inflation Rate				
	3%	5%	7%	9%	11%
5	85,873	77,378	69,569	62,403	55,841
10	73,742	59,874	48,398	38,942	31,182
15	63,325	46,329	33,670	24,301	17,412
20	54,379	35,849	23,424	15,164	9,723
25	46,697	27,739	16,296	9,463	5,429
30	40,101	21,464	11,337	5,905	3,032

Those two charts illustrate why inflation is such an insidious problem for anyone trying to accumulate or to preserve what's been accumulated. It's the underlying reason for the financial fear common among retired people living in the world's most-affluent culture ever. If you feel secure, you probably don't understand inflation!

Figure 10.3
What it will take to buy what $100,000
buys today assuming various inflation rates

At End of Year	Inflation Rate				
	3%	5%	7%	9%	11%
5	115,927	127,628	140,255	153,862	168,506
10	134,392	162,889	196,715	236,736	283,942
15	155,797	207,893	275,903	364,248	478,459
20	180,611	265,330	386,968	560,441	806,231
25	209,378	338,635	542,743	862,308	1,358,546
30	242,726	432,194	761,226	1,326,768	2,289,230

Figure 10.4 illustrates how long an investment fund that earned 10 percent per year would last. For example, beginning with a fund of $100,000, you could withdraw $10,608 per year for thirty years, or a total of $318,240, before the orig-

Figure 10.4
How much you can withdraw per year
before exhausting a retirement fund
(assumes 10% investment growth rate)

Beginning Amount	Time period of withdrawals					
	5 years	10 years	15 years	20 years	25 years	30 years
50,000	13,190	8,137	6,574	5,873	5,508	5,304
100,000	26,380	16,275	13,147	11,746	11,017	10,608
150,000	39,570	24,412	19,721	17,619	16,525	15,912
200,000	52,759	32,549	26,295	23,492	22,034	21,216
250,000	65,949	40,686	32,868	29,365	27,542	26,520
300,000	79,139	48,824	39,442	35,238	33,050	31,824
350,000	92,329	56,961	46,016	41,111	38,559	37,128
400,000	105,519	65,098	52,590	46,984	44,067	42,432
450,000	118,709	73,235	59,163	52,857	49,576	47,736
500,000	131,899	81,373	65,737	58,730	55,084	53,040

inal funds were exhausted. We hope this chart gives you some comfort. If you've accumulated some retirement funds, if you've invested them so as to earn 10 percent before taxes, and if you need to make withdrawals from those funds, you can see how long they'll last.

If you continue to work after age sixty-five or have other sources of income (e.g., Social Security or a pension fund), you may never have to withdraw from your retirement fund at all. That would mean you may never have a possibility of running out of money.

If you had a retirement fund of $100,000 at age sixty-five, for example, but didn't need to withdraw from it at all for ten years (until you were seventy-five), the fund would then be worth $259,374 (assuming it continued to grow at 10% per year). Your life expectancy would also have been decreased by ten years.

Thus, figure 10.5 illustrates that beginning at age seventy-five, you could withdraw $29,365 per year for twenty years before the fund would be exhausted. That compares to being able to withdraw only $10,608 per year for thirty years beginning at age sixty-five (out of the original $100,000 fund). In other words, by not using the fund for ten years, you have increased your payout from approximately $10,000 to $30,000 per year.

Figure 10.5

How much an investment fund will grow
in value assuming a 10% rate of return

Beginning Amount	Investment Time Horizon				
	5 years	10 years	15 years	20 years	25 years
50,000	80,526	129,687	208,862	336,375	541,735
100,000	161,051	259,374	417,725	672,750	1,083,471
150,000	241,577	389,061	626,587	1,009,125	1,625,206
200,000	322,102	518,748	835,450	1,345,500	2,166,941
250,000	402,628	648,436	1,044,312	1,681,875	2,708,676
300,000	483,153	778,123	1,253,174	2,018,250	3,250,412
350,000	563,679	907,810	1,462,037	2,354,625	3,792,147
400,000	644,204	1,037,497	1,670,899	2,691,000	4,333,882
450,000	724,730	1,167,184	1,879,762	3,027,375	4,875,618
500,000	805,255	1,296,871	2,088,624	3,363,750	5,417,353

Clearly, a big variable in retirement planning is your life expectancy. Most people assume that's seventy-five years, so that if you retire at age sixty-five, you have ten years left to provide for. The reality is, however, that the older you get, the longer your life expectancy becomes in terms of total years lived. A large percentage of the American population dies before reaching age sixty-four. Therefore, those who live to age sixty-five have a different life expectancy from someone being born today. At age sixty-five, most men will live to their mid or late eighties, and most women to their late eighties or early nineties. If you've reached age seventy-five and are in good health, you can realistically expect to reach the nineties.

In the last chapter, we talked about caring for aging parents, and that's still a relevant topic in this season of life. According to several studies, as many as 60 percent of the dependent elderly live with adult children. Those of you who reach age sixty-five may have elderly parents move in with you. You may have had an empty nest for a few years, but it may become full again after you retire. And caring for aged parents can be costly, especially if you haven't prepared for it.

Another common concern as people grow older is providing for health care or long-term nursing care. Statistically, the chances of needing long-term nursing care are only about 8 percent for women and 5 percent for men. Of course, probabilities mean nothing if you need the care, and you must plan for that possibility.

As you can see, determining how much is enough involves many variables, probably including some (such as your health) unique to your situation. You may be fearful in this regard. But with good planning, you can probably accumulate enough. For a child of God, however, real peace of mind comes from knowing He has promised throughout the Bible to provide for His own. That is the ultimate in financial security.

How to Take a Pension

Two decisions that are often difficult but crucial when planning to retire are when to start taking Social Security and how to take pension benefits. We'll cover the pension question here and the Social Security issue in the next section.

Using the charts and the process outlined above, first determine whether you need to take *any* benefits from your pension plan. If you don't, you're better off rolling the money into an IRA and not making any withdrawals until age seventy and one-half (when the law says you *have* to start withdrawing). That way, your money will continue to grow tax deferred.

Assuming you need your pension benefits, however, the next best alternative is to take only a portion and roll the amount not needed into an IRA. The amount

> *F*or a child of God, real peace of mind comes from knowing He has promised throughout the Bible to provide for His own. That's the ultimate in financial security.

taken out will be taxed, but it can be withdrawn over your life expectancy, a specified period of time or even in a lump sum.

Those amounts not rolled into an IRA but taken in a lump sum can receive special tax treatment called "ten year forward averaging." A discussion of the way that works is beyond the scope of this book; consult your accountant or other tax adviser for details on how you might benefit.

Sequentially, then, your best option is to not take the pension benefits at retirement but wait as long as possible; the second best is to keep the amounts received as small as possible; the third best is to take only a portion of the plan in regular installments, deferring the balance until a later date. Last, take a lump sum distribution of the entire plan, but use special tax rules.

As always, of course, your cash flow requirements are the determining factor. You probably don't enjoy paying taxes on your pension benefits, but having to pay tax only means your plan has earned income for you. Thus, taxes shouldn't be resented, just planned for.

Social Security

Three questions are commonly asked about Social Security benefits: Will the system survive? When should I take my benefits? And what are my benefits projected to be?

The first question, while a real concern, is out of our hands. The Social Security system was designed to provide only a *supplemental* income for retirees. Over the years, however, it has become a political sacred cow, and Congress has promised the system will provide far more. We should plan as much as possible for our retirement *exclusive of* Social Security; if it's available, fine, but if it's not available, that's fine, too. It may be impossible for you to retire without Social Security, and that's not wrong, but your old age will be more secure if you can plan to retire without it.

We doubt the system will ever go bankrupt, because the political damage would be too great for whichever party was in office. The system can always be kept solvent through higher taxes.

The question of when to take Social Security benefits is relatively easy to answer. If you have the option of taking benefits at age sixty-two rather than waiting until age sixty-five, you're always better off to do so. This is true even though you'll get reduced benefits at the younger age. The total amount of money received from ages sixty-two to sixty-five is large enough that waiting to take bigger benefits will never pay off.

That doesn't mean, however, that you should necessarily retire early so you can take benefits at age sixty-two. If you work for those additional three years, you'll probably be far better off financially, since your income will likely be significantly more than what Social Security would provide.

What you can count on from Social Security depends on two variables: whether or not you've had at least forty "quarters of coverage"—basically ten years of making Social Security payments in even a minimal amount—and how much you've earned and paid into Social Security over your working life. If you earned as little as $2,000 that was taxed for Social Security purposes in a year, you received four quarters of coverage for that year, even if all the money was earned in one quarter. It's easy to satisfy the forty-quarters-of-coverage requirement.

As for the amount you earned, realize that not all income is subject to Social Security tax. The maximum amount of income taxed has varied over the years from as low as $3,000 to as high as the current $53,100. In other words, in 1991, only the first $53,100 of income is taxed for Social Security purposes; any income above that is not subject to Social Security tax.

The point is that many people will qualify for the maximum Social Security benefits. The current maximum for an individual is approximately $950 per month, plus a benefit equal to 50 percent for a nonworking spouse. Therefore, if a retired spouse receives $950 in monthly benefits and the nonworking spouse is the same age, he or she will receive $475 per month, for a total family benefit of $1,425.

The benefits go to the one who earned those benefits. So if both a husband and wife work and only one retires at age sixty-five (having qualified for full benefits), that person will receive full benefits even while the spouse continues to work.

You can receive full benefits only if no salary or income is being earned. If you choose to continue working, you can lose some or all of the monthly benefits, depending on the amount earned.

It's relatively easy to determine what your own Social Security account looks like. You simply fill out and return form SSA-7004-PC, which can be obtained by calling 1-800-234-5772. You'll get back a statement showing your earnings record, your quarters of coverage and your benefits if you retire early, retire at the normal age of sixty-five or delay retirement to age seventy.

Some Social Security benefits may be taxable depending on whether you earn income in retirement from taxable sources. For example, earnings from investments, while not counting as salaried income, could subject some benefits to taxation.

To summarize, don't plan your retirement around Social Security. Take your benefits as early as possible, but don't retire for the sole purpose of receiving benefits. Continuing to work beyond retirement age may be wise as well as necessary. In planning for Social Security benefits, both the amount received and its taxability are unique to your individual circumstances. And as at every other stage of life, planning ahead is essential for achieving the peace of mind that comes from knowing where you are and where you're going.

Preserving Investments

Ron's father retired more than ten years ago. He had worked as a foreman in a factory, been mayor of his city and worked for the state government. He had saved some money, but not enough by any means to make him financially independent at retirement. From the time he retired, he asked Ron's counsel occasionally on where he should invest his money. Ron was hesitant to give advice, because he knew he was dealing with the financial fruit of his parents' fifty years of work. While it wasn't a large sum of money, it certainly was large to them, representing whatever financial security they might have over the rest of their lives.

Eventually, however (in 1987), Ron began to give them specific investment advice. Consistent with the philosophy of taking a long-term perspective, diversifying investments and using professional management, he advised them to put a portion of their money in three different no-load mutual funds.

You may recall that through most of 1987, the stock market went up dramatically almost every day, and people were anxious to participate lest they miss out on a great opportunity. From January to August, the stock market appreciated more than 30 percent in value, and in August Ron's parents finally invested in the funds he had recommended. They put $10,000 in each fund.

On Monday, October 19, 1987, the stock market experienced its greatest one-day crash ever. Ron remembers well the uncertainty, fear, confusion and chagrin of many investors that day. The first call he received the next day was from his parents, wanting to know what to do. As he had thought and prayed on the nineteenth about what to say to anyone, let alone his parents, he still believed in the philosophy we had adopted and he consistently recommends. So his counsel on that Tuesday to his parents and clients was to do nothing, because the original investment decision was still correct.

The stock market continued to decline in October, November and December, and in December it hit its lowest point. Over those months, Ron received frequent calls from his parents. His counsel continued to be the same as before.

In December 1987, his dad told him he wanted to sell two of the mutual funds because the decline in value was causing his mother tremendous anxiety. He subsequently sold the two funds and put the money back into a money market fund. In January 1988, the stock market, quite unexpectedly, began what in retrospect was a two-year increase in value. By the end of January, most of the losses of the preceding October had been fully recovered. The mutual funds Ron had recommended regained all their lost value during January. We relate this true story, not to be critical of Ron's parents, but to illustrate the fear many people experience.

People make two common investing mistakes when they reach retirement age. First, they do nothing with their investments, leaving them as they had been invested in the company they worked for: cash, money market accounts or whatever vehicles had been used to accumulate those retirement assets. Second, they tend to shorten their perspective and move toward income-producing assets and investments that are cash or near-cash types. The motivation for those decisions or nondecisions is the fear of losing their retirement savings.

A caution is in order here, however. If you're dependent on all your investments to provide income for your retirement, you *can't* risk stock market ups and downs. You must take a very conservative approach and maintain your investments in income-producing, safe instruments. Investing in anything that may go down in value just when you need that money is too risky. The long-term perspective and diversification are for those who have some portion of their investments that they should still be setting aside to grow in value over a long period.

Assuming you're able to continue taking a long-term perspective with at least some of your retirement funds, realize risks are involved because the economy goes through cycles. The long-term trend of the market has been steadily positive, however, and with some basic investment knowledge you can minimize the risks. We strongly encourage you to read chapter 17 for a discussion of the keys to investment success.

Continuing Life Insurance Need

You'll probably want to continue with a life insurance program after retirement for two reasons. First, the cash value insurance you purchased many years ago may turn out to be a very good investment vehicle, because the cash values continue to grow tax deferred—they won't be taxed until you cancel the policy.

Second, you're likely to live for another twenty years or more. If you do and your estate continues to grow, your heirs could be left with a significant estate tax problem.

For example, if you and your husband have assets of $250,000 at age sixty-five (including your home) and you live for twenty more years, with those assets increasing in value at 10 percent per year, you'll have an estate of almost $1,681,000 at age eighty-five. The taxes due on that size estate will be several hundred thousand dollars. To pay for them will require not only good planning, but probably the use of some life insurance as well. And in that case, the life insurance you took out many years ago may be the best purchase you ever made.

Chapter 15 describes in detail how to determine your life insurance needs. It also explains the differences between term and whole-life insurance. The insurance problem most often created in retirement is not having enough coverage at a time when the cost of new insurance, because of your age, skyrockets. Buying term life insurance at this stage may be prohibitively expensive. Again, chapter 15 will help you determine how much insurance you need and which product would be best for you.

Preparing for Your Husband's Death

Contemplating your husband's death isn't pleasant, but as we said earlier, seven of ten wives will be widowed, so it's a probability you can't afford to ignore. You don't want to end up like the woman described in an article in the *Money* magazine of June 1988. Thirty-six-year-old Jude Okney's lawyer-husband died and left her to care for their three children in 1986. He was seriously underinsured, and only Social Security and a trust fund created after his death by a group of friends allowed Jude to keep up the payments on their house. She had always left the family finances to her husband, but now, in the midst of her grief, she had to handle the estate, assume financial control of the household, and even close the untidy books on her husband's law practice. "If only Bruce had taken 10 minutes one day to write out where things were," she lamented.

A happily contrasting story involves a good friend and client of our firm who has prepared for his wife a large notebook with an index, tabs and copies of everything he thinks she may need in the event of his death. His level of preparation for his death is rare, but we strongly recommend it for every married couple. (A booklet giving the details is available from Crown Ministries Inc., 530 Crown Oak Centre Dr., Longwood, FL 32750; (407) 331-6000.) At the very least, you and your husband should discuss, and you should know where to find, each of the following:

1. Listing of all assets.

2. Listing of all debts and repayment schedules.

3. The most-recent family budget.

4. Listing and location of all important documents, including insurance policies, company benefit plan descriptions, investments, deeds, funeral plot deed and wills; location of safe deposit box.

5. Funeral desires.

6. Names, addresses and telephone numbers of people who should be notified upon the death of your husband.

7. Location of any financial plan or estate plans that have been prepared.

8. Names, addresses and telephone numbers of all important advisers, as well as a summary of everything that's been discussed with them relative to financial and estate planning.

Lastly, you and your husband should discuss the financial issues of your remarriage. Ron used to have a client whose husband died and left her financially comfortable. She was very lonely, and for some social contact she started taking dance lessons. She met an instructor who had been divorced twice and had never held a responsible job for any length of time. He had no financial assets of his own when Ron's client met him.

Obviously, her friends saw many indications of potential danger in that relationship, but the woman chose to marry the man without benefit of any counsel from advisers or friends. She merely announced her marriage after the fact.

The woman immediately transferred title to all her assets to her new husband and terminated all professional relationships. About a year later, Ron got a call from her. She tearfully asked what she could do, as her whole life had become a nightmare. Her marriage had turned into a disaster, and her husband had total control over her and all the property she and her first husband had accumulated in a lifetime of work. At that point, of course, it was impossible to do anything, and she was committed to living out the rest of her life in an unhappy marriage or else giving up at least half her assets.

In chapter 9, we described the situation of Judy's mother and her second husband and now his third wife. Such a situation raises property questions and inheritance questions.

The property questions are different in a second marriage compared to a first marriage. As a widow, you have some responsibilities to a deceased husband and your children from that marriage. You and your husband should discuss what will happen to any specific property the two of you have accumulated. What provision should be made for the various children and grandchildren? There isn't necessarily one, right answer; discussing that ahead of time will ease the dilemma you may face without him there to counsel you.

Conclusion

To finish the story of Ron's parents, they did not lose all their life savings, only a portion. They're typical of retired people in that they live as frugally in retirement as they did throughout their life. As a result, their assets continue to grow in retirement.

Concern about being able to live as well in the future as you do today is legitimate. Ron's professional observation, however, is that most people, when they reach retirement age, have established such good disciplines of life and have prepared well enough for retirement that they tend to live *better* than they did in any other season of their lives.

Concern about having to meet major health-care needs is also legitimate and must be planned for. You may need to help your aging parents, as we discussed in the preceding chapter, or you may come to need the assistance of your own children.

Our final challenge to those who retire is to ask again the key question: Is retirement work's end or a second wind? Planning in this season revolves around investment questions and having enough to last the rest of your life. Never forget, however, that financial planning won't provide ultimate security or freedom. Those come only from our heavenly Father.

CHAPTER ELEVEN

Single Again: Widowhood

*I*n June 1988, a group of men spent three days together at a beautiful retreat setting in Montana. They planned, prayed and dreamed together about the future. When they left that retreat, they were committed to one another and to being the godly leaders and husbands they knew the Lord wanted them to be.

One of the men was a pilot, and he invited three of the others to fly back to Dallas with him. One of the four was an entrepreneur with a young wife and two boys below the age of five. Another was a banker who had three boys, one of whom was in high school and two of whom were in college. The third was a surgeon with three grown children, and the fourth was a pastor who also had three children.

The small plane took off all right, but en route to Dallas it disappeared. Several days later, when the wreckage was found, there were no survivors. In an instant, four women had become widows, and eleven children were left without a father.

Ron visited with one of the widows many months later, and she said her husband had always told her that in the event of his death, she needn't worry because his best friend knew all about their financial situation. He was well prepared to help her cope financially with his death. Unfortunately, however, that friend had been one of the other three men on the plane.

Death is rarely expected, so rarely do people plan for it adequately. Yet when it occurs, it changes forever the financial lives of those left behind (as well as every other aspect of their lives).

Life situations are continually changing. Children grow up, investments do well or poorly, job promotions may occur, moves are made to different homes and different parts of the country—even your friends and relatives can grow closer or drift away. And past plans about the death of your husband may not be relevant today because of those changing circumstances.

Seventy percent of all married women will experience widowhood. The statistics are meaningless if it happens to you, of course, because then it's 100 percent for you. And if it occurs, it will likely take you by surprise.

Widows usually have three immediate questions:

1. What do I need to do when?
2. Whom can I trust to advise me?
3. Will I be able to live as well in the future as I have in the past?

In this chapter, we want to answer those questions and outline some steps you can take to prepare for widowhood if you're not already a widow. We also want to cover briefly some of the financial issues related to remarriage.

What to Do When

Elizabeth Mooney wrote an article for the *Washington Post* several years ago in which she described how her husband had tried to "protect" her from his impending death, leaving her totally unprepared to deal with widowhood. Until he died in her arms, she was convinced he would recover his health.

She continued: "It takes two years, say the psychiatrists, before a widow absorbs what has happened and is capable of making decisions. Early, there is the merciful numbness, the long weeks before you, as a survivor of the amputation, feel the real cut of the knife. . . . [L]ittle by little you realize that everything from taxes and insurance to the unsticking of windows and the changing of furnace filters is up to you, and nobody is even going to remind you."

Because of that two-year period of psychological adjustment, Ron advises all his clients who are widows to not make any major financial decisions during that time. However, the fear of being unable to maintain their standard of living often drives them to make financial decisions too soon. In many cases, they make the wrong decisions.

One client's husband was killed in an accident, and she received a fairly large wrongful-death settlement that should have made her financially independent for the rest of her life. She had no knowledge of money matters, however, and turned to a friend for investment counsel. She was advised to make some specific investments, including the purchase of a seven-bedroom house, even though she had only two children left at home. When she came to us, she was living alone in that huge house and had no cash reserves.

You must make some decisions, of course, but be careful about making any big choices immediately. Below are the steps we recommend you follow in the first two years and beyond.

Immediately

First look for funeral directions left by your husband. They may be found in his will, in a separate letter or perhaps in a file the two of you discussed.

Second, order (from either the funeral director or the county clerk's office) ten to twenty certified copies of the death certificate. This needs to be done right after the funeral in order to claim the benefits due you from company pension plans, Social Security, life insurance proceeds and so on. You'll also need the documentary proof of your husband's death to change titles on cars and your home.

Third, arrange for someone to stay at your home during the funeral to protect your property. Unfortunately, unscrupulous people prey upon widows, and a favorite ploy is to burglarize a home during a funeral.

Within the First Two Weeks

Have your attorney review your husband's will and file it in probate court if necessary. Collect any documents needed to claim death benefits (bank and brokerage statements, marriage certificate, birth certificate). Contact your insurance agent, spouse's employer and former employers and the Social Security office to start the process of claiming benefits due you.

Within One Month

Keep a record of your cash flow so you can determine where you stand financially and what your living expenses are likely to be.

As money from insurance or employers begins to come in, deposit it in a bank in short-term certificates of deposit (CDs) or money market funds. One strategy is to put the money equally into six, twelve, eighteen and twenty-four month CDs so that you'll have money coming available to you every six months. At this point it's not necessary to worry about missing out on "better" investment opportunities. What you primarily need to do now is ensure you can pay your bills as they arise over the next twenty-four months.

Within the First Six Months

Change any of *your* insurance policies that name your deceased spouse as beneficiary. Change any joint billing and credit card accounts that have your husband's name on them. If you are the executor of your husband's estate, notify your creditors and satisfy the debts as they come due. If there are likely to be estate taxes, get professional advice to determine how much they'll be and when they'll be due.

Review all insurance coverage, especially medical insurance, to make sure you and your family are adequately protected. Have your will revised to reflect the changed circumstances. You may need to appoint a guardian for your young children or change the executor or trustee, since your husband has most likely been named as executor and trustee in your will.

Review your husband's checkbook and files to determine if you may be due benefits from sources you didn't know about before: a union, fraternal organization, credit life insurance, military benefits or other life insurance policies.

The Second Year

In the second year, you should begin to develop short- and long-term financial plans. Major investment decisions still do not need to be made, but it's time to do the following:

1. List all the assets you now have.
2. List all debts.

3. List all the life insurance covering you.

4. List all sources of income.

5. List all your expenses, categorized by major area.

6. List all insurance policies.

7. Begin thinking about and listing some long-term, major needs such as college education, life-style needs, debt payoff, giving and so on.

*D*elay making major life-style and investment decisions for two years.

In the third year and beyond, you should start to implement your financial plan, making decisions about investments, insurance and life-style.

While this is the approach we recommend, it's not written in concrete, and you should tailor it to your unique situation. Depending on your personality, training, age and income level, the sequence and time frame you follow may differ.

We do strongly encourage you, however, to delay making major life-style and investment decisions for approximately two years; you need that time to adjust to the death of a significant part of your life.

Whom Can You Trust to Advise You?

Recently we received a letter asking the following question: "I am a widow with a teenage son. Several years ago I switched the insurance settlement from my husband's death from certificates of deposit in my local bank to a brokerage firm managed by a friend in our church. Now that friend has left the firm, the business is in trouble with lawsuits against it, and we have lost over $4,000. What advice can you give me?"

Chapter 14 deals with the actual process of choosing a financial adviser. But for now we want to offer four thoughts regarding such a choice.

First, we recommend you choose a personal adviser, not necessarily a financial adviser. What you need at this point is not technical advice but wisdom and judgment. Money management skills can be purchased later.

Don't expect to find technical expertise in all areas of finance in any one individual. Just because someone is a CPA, attorney, banker, broker, life insurance agent or financial planner doesn't make the person knowledgeable in all the areas where you may need advice.

Second, don't choose advisers just because they're Christians, family members, friends or men. Those may be important factors to consider, but again, what you need are wisdom, judgment and perhaps experience. If you're taking an airplane trip, you want a pilot who has the skills, training, experience and wisdom to make the right decisions. You wouldn't choose a pilot merely because the person is a Christian, family member, friend or man. In the same way, it may be that another widow would be your best personal adviser or could at least direct you to other helpers. You might also ask your pastor for recommendations.

Third, you may want more than one personal adviser. Perhaps you *do* want a family member, friend, Christian and/or male to advise you, but it's biblical to seek the advice of more than one counselor.

Fourth, always remember that you're still the decision maker. You can't abdicate that responsibility, even if you receive bad advice. Seek the best counsel you can find, and then rely on the wisdom, comfort and encouragement of the Holy Spirit to guide you during this difficult period of adjustment.

Will I Be Able to Live As Well in the Future?

Doubt about the future strikes every new widow at a time when her security has been greatly shaken. Many fears and questions arise. We can answer the questions fairly objectively, but as a widow you need far more than objective answers. If you've had no experience in managing money, even $1 million of life insurance may feel inadequate.

We would encourage you to go back and reread the first four chapters of this book to help you understand the basics of money management. Realizing that God owns it all and provides all the resources you will ever need should help you overcome some of the fear.

Whether or not you'll be able to live as well in the future is determined by three things: your income, expenses and long-term needs. We also know that when you prepare a financial plan, peace of mind will come from knowing either what steps you have to take to get your house in order or that you really are perfectly okay financially.

We offer three rules for a widow in preparing a financial plan: Keep it simple, keep it flexible, and make it yours and not someone else's. These are the elements of a good financial plan: determine what you owe, what you own, what your income is, what your expenses are, what your long-term needs are and the amount of insurance you have; keep your will current; provide all the medical and liability insurance your circumstances dictate.

You will receive income from several sources. Insurance proceeds can be taken either in a lump sum, which we generally recommend, or as a monthly income for the rest of your life. The lump sum is preferable because the monthly payout may not keep up with inflation. By taking the money all at once and investing it yourself, you have more control over the results.

The second source of income is salaries and wages either from salary continuation plans your husband may have had or, more likely, your own ability to work.

Your husband's former employers may have pension plans that will provide you either regular income or lump-sum payments. Your age, the amount in the plan and your needs will determine which way is the best to take those payments, but again, lump sums are generally preferable for the reasons given above.

Social Security will provide some benefits for widows who have children under the ages of eighteen or nineteen. It will also benefit widows over the age of sixty-two. Your local Social Security office can answer questions about the benefits to which you're entitled.

If you're a widow with children below the ages of eighteen or nineteen and receive Social Security benefits, those benefits will be reduced for income you earn. The benefits will stop altogether at the time your youngest child finishes high school, then begin again when you reach age sixty-two. How much you receive will depend on how much you and your husband paid into the Social Security fund.

Some of the less-obvious sources of income mentioned earlier in the chapter—fraternal organizations, unions and perhaps the military—may also provide certain benefits for you as a widow.

Once you add up all the sources of income, you've completed the first significant step in determining whether you'll be able to live as well in the future as you have in the past.

The second major step is to calculate what your expenses will be. That will take some time, as many things will be changing. Most couples assume that if they have an income of $40,000 and are saving no money, the wife would continue to need $40,000 to maintain her life-style as a widow. That's not the case; expenses such as food, clothing and transportation will go down.

Another big consideration is that you're now the sole decision maker when it comes to spending money. The way you spend may be different from how you and your husband together spent money. By completing the forms at the end of

*I*t's more important for a widow or single parent to have a will than it is for a married couple.

chapter 4, you can begin the process of determining how much you'll need to live. Revise those estimates every six months for the first two or three years until you have a good understanding of what your life-style will be.

If you weren't doing it before, you'll now need to reconcile your monthly bank statements. In the process, you'll be reviewing how you're spending money, and you'll have a greater sense of control over your financial situation. At first you may feel *less* secure because you understand better how much money is being spent without the provision of your husband's regular income. Over time, however, you should begin to feel more control and security.

The third major factor determining your standard of living is your long-term major needs. Make a list of those needs, the dates when they're needed and the estimated amount that will be needed. Typical needs include college education for your kids, debt payoff and life-style needs such as replacement of cars and home repairs. Committing the needs to paper will begin to give you a sense of control and security, because you eliminate the anxiety of the unknown.

Another concern doesn't really deal with life-style, but you need to have an updated, appropriate will. It's more important for a widow or single parent to have a will, in fact, than it is for a married couple. This is especially true if you have young children. The likelihood of both parents' dying at the same time is slim compared to the likelihood of a single parent's dying.

For the same reason, life insurance also becomes a key consideration. If you're a single parent and don't have enough financial resources, it's vital that you provide for your kids through insurance on your life.

Life insurance may be appropriate as well to meet estate tax needs. This is a professional question that can be answered by an insurance adviser or financial planner. Whether you need life insurance (and if so, how much) depends on your unique family and financial situation.

Early on, you'll need to make sure you have medical insurance coverage. Chapter 16 should help you make the necessary decisions. Major health problems can destroy your ability to provide for your family. Thus, good insurance is essential.

The last issue affecting how well you'll be able to live is the whole area of investments. Life insurance proceeds or investments your husband left you may be your primary source of income. How that money is invested is extremely important to your long-term financial security. Chapter 17 describes investing in depth and should help you think through the decisions you'll face. But you'll probably also need some type of professional help in making your investment decisions. Chapter 14 will guide you in selecting those advisers.

Always remember that *every investment carries some risk,* and generally speaking, the higher the rate of return you're seeking, the greater the risk you're taking. You can minimize risk in two ways. First, take a long-term perspective on your investing, and don't try to get in and out of investments as markets change. Second, make sure your investments are well diversified so that when one goes down, as it most certainly will, others will provide stability.

Conclusion

We were visiting one of the widows described at the start of this chapter. It had been more than two years since her husband died in the plane crash. She has had a significant ministry around the country sharing some of her challenges as a widow. Her life has been no easier than that of other widows, but she turned the tragedy into an outreach to others in similar circumstances.

As we talked with her, she raised an interesting point. "After these last several years," she said, "I have reached an identity crisis. Who am I? Am I to be forever my husband's widow, or am I a unique person? I do not want to make a career out of widowhood."

In saying that, she expressed considerable insight into one of the keys to building a new life, and that's determining who you are and what you want to be. The inescapable facts are that more than 70 percent of the married women you know will experience widowhood and that the life expectancy of women is considerably longer than generally thought. You may very well live to be ninety years old or even older. God has given you experiences that build wisdom if interpreted and used correctly. And that wisdom can be a tremendous benefit to others who will go through the same dark valleys.

CHAPTER TWELVE

Going It Alone:
Single Parent

*K*aren Loritts is a regular speaker at Campus Crusade's Family Life Conferences. She recently wrote an article for *Worldwide Challenge* magazine in which she said, "The phone rang, jarring me from sleep.

"The teary voice on the other end of the line was my dear friend, calling long distance. We have a close friendship; she is the sister I never had. We have talked, prayed together, studied the Word and enjoyed family times together.

"As it turned out, she was in distress over the imminent death of her 10-year marriage. 'Lord, what words of comfort do You have?' was my whispered prayer. I felt her pain and cried at the prospect of having my friend struggle with this 'death.'

"The couple, from all outward appearances, seemed to have an ideal marriage. Her husband worked hard and involved the family in Christian ministry; she worked full time at home with her two beautiful children—nurturing them in the Scriptures and loving her family sacrificially. Under the surface, however, serious problems existed in their relationship, and their marriage deteriorated.

"Several months passed before the divorce decree was granted. By the stroke of a pen on a document, she is now a divorcée, a single parent and the head of her household. She now lives in a world unfamiliar to her, on a journey she was unprepared to travel."

According to the U.S. Census Bureau and the National Center for Health Statistics, the following things are true of single-parent families:

In 1960, 5 million children were being raised by mothers who were widowed, divorced, separated or never married. By 1988, the number of children had risen to 13.5 million.

In 1940, 3.5 percent of U.S. births were to unwed women, and even in 1960 the proportion was only 5.3 percent. Births to unmarried women have since soared, however, to 22 percent of total births in 1985 (the latest count). Focus on the Family's Family Research Council puts the figure as high as 25 percent.

Seventy percent of married women will experience widowhood, and the average age of the widow is fifty-two.

Fifty percent of all marriages will end in divorce.

The percentage of children living with their mothers only has increased steadily: 10.8 percent in 1970; 18 percent in 1980; 20.9 percent in 1985; 21.4 percent in 1988.

The number of widowed, divorced and never married mothers is also climbing: 2.86 million in 1970; 5.45 million in 1980; 6.01 million in 1985; 6.27 million in 1988.

Clearly, more than 50 percent of American households with children will be headed by single parents (mostly mothers) at some point. And unfortunately, the divorce statistics are about the same for Christians and non-Christians.

Comparison of Widowhood and Divorce

Most divorced women, like widows, have little time to get ready financially for the adjustment. It's noteworthy that Karen Loritts characterized her friend's divorce as "my friend's struggle with this 'death.'"

Newly divorced and widowed women face the same three questions: What do I need to do when? Whom can I trust as an adviser? Will I be able to live as well in the future as I have in the past? Answers to those questions make up the bulk of this chapter.

Another similarity in both cases is that you, the survivor, are left as the primary decision maker in all areas of your family's life, including the financial questions. That burden is very real.

Many other similarities exist between widowhood and divorce, but there are also significant differences. For one, divorce will almost certainly be more difficult financially. You've not only lost most or all of your spouse's income as a support to the family, but you also don't have the life insurance proceeds or Social Security benefits a widow has.

Statistics show that a divorced mother has only 40 percent of the income that used to come into the household. Child-rearing expenses will be just as great—maybe even higher if the woman was a homemaker and now has to get a job and pay for child care—but the income is 60 percent less than before. Obviously, that kind of income drop makes paying the bills very difficult. Some single moms, desperate to avoid the cost of child care, go off to work leaving their small children home alone.

We believe the feminist movement may have contributed to this disparity, as the courts are far less lenient in granting benefits to a divorced woman than they were prior to the movement's advent. The courts now consider women equal to men in earning ability. The reality, however, is that most women don't have the same earning potential as their ex-husbands.

Financial Consequences of Divorce

We know a couple who have three teenage children. They went through a divorce several years ago. The woman has been a teacher for many years. Unlike many other single parents, she has a profession she can rely on. The divorce was prompted largely by the husband's inability to maintain a steady job. He never could support the family adequately, which is why she always worked. Together they struggled with debts and inadequate income for the needs of a growing family.

Ron has received many letters over the years from women who relate the stresses brought about by the poor financial decisions of their husbands. One lady wrote that her husband's attitude toward debt was so stressful to her that she

"had to legally cut [her] ties." Her fear was that she was going to lose all financial security.

Those letters and the story of our friend demonstrate that financial problems
often contribute to divorce. In fact, more than 50 percent of the people who
divorce indicate that financial problems fostered the breakup. Those problems
may be only symptomatic of others, but they clearly add to the strain the family
is under.

This typically means single mothers face both a limited income and debts carried over from the failed marriage. They're often in a far less secure financial
position than even when the marriage began. In addition, there are potentially
high costs associated with the divorce itself.

Besides legal costs, there are also tax consequences to a divorce. If you receive
alimony, that money is taxable income to you. Perhaps the home has had to be
sold as part of the divorce settlement. If the proceeds are not reinvested in another
home, which they probably can't be, there will be capital gains taxes to pay.

For all those reasons, a divorced mother is usually dealing with day-to-day
cash flow concerns, whereas a widow is generally dealing with investment and
planning questions. In addition, the divorcée has the emotional strain of a relationship with an ex-husband.

What to Do When

Like a widow, a divorced woman faces enormous psychological, emotional
and financial adjustments. Therefore, if you go through divorce, *you should give*

*T*he primary way to reduce the cost of
divorce is to avoid contentiousness.

yourself at least two years before making any major investment or financial
planning decisions. Obviously, day-to-day concerns have to be taken care of, but
choices like when and where to move, estate plans and investment decisions (if

any) should be delayed. A woman does need to do certain things to protect herself during a divorce, however, and we outline them below.

Before the Divorce Becomes Final

Please understand that we're *not* advocating divorce. God hates divorce (see Mal. 2:16), and so should we. Marriage vows are taken far too lightly today; when couples say "Till death do us part," what they often mean is "Till we don't *feel* in love anymore." We need to take more seriously the warning of Deuteronomy 23:23: "Whatever your lips utter you must be sure to do, because you made your vow freely to the Lord your God with your own mouth." The commitment to love in spite of feelings and circumstances is essential to upholding a marriage through thick and thin, and reconciliation should always be our goal if it's at all possible.

We have to acknowledge, however, that couples do divorce, even Christians, and say that if it appears to be a definite possibility in your case, you need to make some appropriate plans. Your goal should not be to "get" your husband or take him for all he's worth, but you should protect yourself and your children.

The first step is to pick a competent and trusted adviser. As we suggested to widows in the preceding chapter, you may want to choose a personal adviser as opposed to a professional adviser at this point. A friend, another woman in a similar situation or the elders at your church may be able to guide you through the process of selecting an attorney to handle your side of the divorce.

The cost of divorce can be prohibitive, as many attorneys charge $150 to $250 per hour. Even a simple, uncontested divorce can cost from several hundred to several thousand dollars depending on how much property is involved.

It's possible to avoid attorneys entirely by using a do-it-yourself divorce kit found in many bookstores. We don't recommend that approach, however, because you could easily overlook crucial details, and your situation may not be as simple you think. Anytime property or children are involved, the situation is complex. Also, each state's divorce and property laws are different. The divorce can be further complicated if you've lived in more than one state or acquired property in more than one state. For the same reasons, you should never attempt to be your own divorce attorney.

The primary way to reduce the cost of divorce is to avoid contentiousness. The more contentious your split, the more expensive it will be. If your husband agrees, you might want to approach a service such as Christian Conciliation Service or some other mediating body that could help reduce the costs and still provide competent advice.

In addition to choosing trusted advisers and legal counsel prior to the divorce, you need to do the following:

1. Establish credit in your own name. It's almost impossible to function in our culture without a credit rating. If credit cards, bank accounts and other accounts are in your husband's name alone, you may have difficulty establishing your own credit. It's therefore advisable to apply for credit in your own name at your bank.

2. List all assets you can find, along with how those assets are titled. This would include investments, cars, furniture, bank accounts and brokerage accounts.

3. Notify banks and brokerage firms—wherever you have joint accounts—of your intention to divorce. Ask both the banker and the broker to allow no transactions in your accounts without written approval by you and your spouse.

4. Close out all joint charge accounts. If you don't and your husband makes charges for whatever amounts, you are jointly as well as individually liable for that debt. Notify the creditors in writing that you're no longer responsible for your spouse's purchases. Creditors may agree to let you keep accounts open in joint names but only be liable for your own purchases.

5. Consider setting up a savings account in your own name so you can have some ready cash if your husband stops contributing to the payment of household bills. You'll probably be liable for all utilities and household expenses if your husband decides to stop making those payments.

6. Make sure you understand the true costs of operating the household. The budget sheets at the end of chapter 4 will help you identify many of the costs. Go through the check registers from the past two or three years and list the expenses by major category. This will help you when it comes to negotiating such terms of divorce as child support and alimony payments. And it will be far less expensive for you to gather the information than to hire an accountant or your attorney to do it.

In addition, you can review prior years' tax returns to get some indication of money spent, investments made and sources of income you may not have known about. The more information you have, the more you're able to assist your attorney in negotiating a fair and reasonable settlement.

The Negotiation Process

The last financial step in divorce, one that could take a long time, is the negotiation process. In that process, all the assets will be divided; the responsibility for debts will be determined; child support amounts will be set; alimony amount and duration will be decided; and lastly and very importantly, visitation rights will be established. How well the negotiation is done will depend not only on the information you provide to your attorney, but also on his or her skill as an advocate for you.

How well the settlement is negotiated will largely determine the tax consequences of the divorce, too. What appears valuable *before* taxes may be far less valuable *after* taxes. For example, any alimony paid to you for at least three years will be deductible to your husband on his tax return and taxable to you as income. The amount can even decline by as much as $15,000 per year.

To illustrate, suppose your ex-husband pays you alimony of $35,000 the first year, $20,000 the second year and $5,000 the third year. He will be able to deduct $60,000 from his tax returns over those three years, and you'll have to report taxable income of $60,000. Thus, your attorney should attempt to increase the amount of alimony paid to take into account the tax benefit your former husband is getting and the tax liability you are assuming.

Property settlements can also have tax consequences. After 1985, all property transferred as part of a divorce settlement is treated as a gift between spouses, so no taxes are paid on the transfer.

That sounds good, but if property (stock, real estate, etc.) is transferred that originally cost $1,000 and now is worth $50,000, you don't have $50,000 available to you. When the property is sold, you will have a taxable gain of $49,000, and those taxes will reduce severely the amount of money available to you. If, on the other hand, property that cost $50,000 is transferred to you and you sell it for $50,000, you have no tax on that gain, so you really do have $50,000. Thus, what specific property is transferred in the divorce settlement can change your cash flow by as much as 40 percent.

Another issue in the property settlement is the family home. If that's transferred to you, you get the benefit of rolling the profits into a new home within two years after its sale, thereby avoiding the capital gains taxes. If, however, the home will be sold to provide you cash, you'll be liable for the capital gain taxes due on the sale. If you're over age fifty-five, of course, you can take advantage of the one-time exclusion of $125,000 of gain on the home when it's ultimately sold.

In negotiating child support, be aware that while it's not taxable income to you, which is good, it's also not deductible for your ex-husband (unlike alimony). That makes it less attractive to him financially if he's paying it.

Another issue relative to child support is who gets to claim exemptions for the children on tax returns. The parent who pays more than 50 percent of the child's support gets the exemption unless the other spouse signs a waiver. So even if your ex-husband provides more than half your child's support, you can still take the exemption if your former spouse will agree to it.

If he is extremely well paid, he should be especially amenable to signing a waiver, because dependent exemptions are being phased out anyway for single taxpayers with incomes over $89,560. If your former husband fits that category, he'll get no benefit from the exemption anyway, so it should be used by you if you're in a lower tax bracket.

This is all a moot issue, of course, if you provide more than half the support of your child, which can be determined by the family budget you've already prepared. In that case, you can just take the exemption on your return and reduce your tax liability accordingly.

Lastly, while the divorce is being negotiated, you need to review the medical insurance coverage you and your children will have. If you need to provide it yourself, chapter 16 will help you make good decisions.

After the Divorce Is Final

After the divorce becomes final and all property transactions are completed, you should have set up your own bank and brokerage accounts, applied for your own credit cards and started functioning on your own. Now, besides living in accordance with a financial plan, you need to rewrite your will and review your children's insurance coverage, which may have been provided by your husband.

Those protections become more critical now than ever, because you may be your kids' sole support. Again, chapter 16 can help with your insurance questions, and an attorney can assist you with the will revision. This step is too important to delay beyond the first few weeks after the divorce is final.

Whom Can I Trust As an Adviser?

Chapter 14 explains how to find a financial adviser. But as we pointed out earlier, your first need may be for a personal adviser rather than a technical counselor. Financial skills can be bought, but you may not be able to purchase wisdom and judgment at any price from a professional adviser.

Second, don't choose someone just because the person is a Christian, family member, friend or male. Men may be able to sympathize with your situation, but they'll never be able to empathize. And being a Christian, relative or friend doesn't necessarily make a person experienced, wise or one who has good judgment.

Third, consider having more than one adviser. The Bible says that multiple counselors help plans to succeed (see Prov. 15:22).

Fourth, regardless of who advises you, you must take responsibility for your decisions. You can't push that off on anyone else. As difficult psychologically and emotionally as divorce is, you can't abdicate your need to make decisions. It's also true that being forced to make decisions may be one of the quickest ways you can recover from the trauma of divorce, since it makes you deal with reality and take the next step.

Will I Be Able to Live As Well?

The financial consequences of divorce on single mothers are often devastating. Two stories came to our attention that make that reality painfully clear.

An article entitled "Suddenly Single" in *Money* magazine (June 1988) included the story of Jane Fox, a mother of two. After her divorce five years earlier, she found that despite having a job, getting $750 per month in child support and having received a five-figure settlement from the sale of a small farm she and her husband had owned, she still could not rent the apartment she wanted. "There

I was," she said, "a grown woman who had co-owned property in the state, being told I couldn't get an apartment on my own merits. I had to go to my father and ask him to cosign the lease. It was insulting."

Fortunately for this woman, after three years of what she called "a dingy, gray little existence," she earned a master's degree in computer science and got a high-paying job. But as the article goes on to say, such a financial recovery is extremely difficult. The article concludes, "Legal fees and the expense of maintaining separate households will almost always lower the standard of living of decoupled couples."

Ron's experience in counseling those who have gone through a divorce concurs—couples rarely do as well separately as they did together. It's important from a biblical perspective, however, to not be resentful, bitter or fearful. Rather, you need to be realistic about where you are financially and what your alternatives are, as well as dependent upon a faithful and all-powerful God.

It's not only younger single mothers who face hardship as a consequence of divorce. An article in *Modern Maturity* (Aug./Sept. 1990) tells of a woman named Donna Spurrier who was looking forward to a worry-free retirement. Her husband of thirty years had always handled their money, but then he suddenly left her.

"I was scared to death," she said. "The worst part was not even knowing if I had enough money to pay the bills." She didn't. "I lost weight because I couldn't afford to buy food and was too proud to go to my family and friends and say 'I'm hungry.'" Her situation got so bad that for a while, she had to work three jobs to keep up the payments on her house and car.

You begin to determine how well you'll be able to live by developing a financial plan as outlined in the first four chapters of this book. You'll confront the same questions, problems and challenges during the various seasons of life that a married couple will face. The primary difference will be that you don't have the financial resources you had as a couple, and therefore you may be forced to choose different alternatives.

During the young-children period of life, for example, you'll be concerned with living on a budget, avoiding debt, maintaining the right life insurance, having a will, deciding how to school your kids, training your children to manage money and choosing whether to buy a house (if that's possible for you) or rent— just like a married couple.

During the teen and college years, you'll be concerned with providing a secondary education for your children. It may be more likely that they'll have to work to pay part of the cost now that household income is reduced. That wouldn't hurt them, of course, and may be God's best way of supplying their college education. What you spend on their cars and weddings will also be affected.

Those are just a few examples. The underlying reality is that you'll almost certainly have to take a more conservative approach to planning and managing your financial life than you did when you were married.

If you're a *widowed* single parent, you'll need to make the same decisions. You'll probably have more money to work with than most divorced mothers, however, so you'll have more options.

One other financial challenge you may face is caring for your aging parents. As a single woman, you may well be called upon to support them, even if you have siblings, just because you don't have a spouse to contend with. That's not necessarily right or fair, but statistics show that three-fourths of those caring for the elderly are women, and the number of elderly being cared for is in the millions. Furthermore, nearly 40 percent of those caring for the elderly are still raising children of their own.

A 1988 U.S. House of Representatives report showed that the average American woman will spend seventeen years raising children and eighteen years

*T*he average American woman will spend seventeen years raising children and eighteen years helping aged parents.

helping aged parents. As people live longer and chronic, disabling conditions become more common, the likelihood increases that your parents will need extra care. And again, this responsibility may fall on you as a single parent.

The financial problem in caring for aging parents is that Medicare generally doesn't cover the costs of the long-term health care so often needed by the elderly. Medicaid will pay for nursing and home care in some states, but it only provides after the parents have used all their assets and become indigent. Many elderly people either use all their life savings caring for themselves or must somehow give away or use all their financial assets in order to establish a need for Medicaid.

The topic of caring for aging parents is broad and difficult and is only partially answered by chapter 16. When they move in with you or you're financially responsible for them, you have to revise the family budget to reflect the increased expenses. There are no easy answers. The only thing you can do is to discuss that possibility ahead of time with your parents and make provisions when everyone is fully competent to do so. Such decisions are always best made ahead of time rather than in the heat of the need. Unfortunately, as with divorce or widowhood, caring for elderly parents is rarely planned for and so usually becomes an unexpected financial emergency that can destroy a family's best-laid plans.

As a single parent, you need to remember that the keys to financial success are very simple regardless of your financial situation. Understand that God owns it all, spend less than you earn, avoid the use of debt, maintain as much liquidity as you can and set some long-term goals. Those may prove difficult to follow, we know, but God is faithful.

CHAPTER THIRTEEN

Career Single

One of the people we respect most is Judy's Aunt Avis. She's close to ninety years old now, has never been married, worked all her adult life as a teacher and has always typified sound money management.

Aunt Avis became a teacher more than sixty-five years ago. She taught in only two school systems, and when she retired in 1975, she owned her home and was caring for an aged mother and a younger sister at her own expense. In addition, she provided so well for her retirement that still today, twenty-five years after retirement, her financial nest egg continues to grow rather than decrease.

She did things right without having the services of a professional financial planner. She spent less than she earned, saved for the future, never borrowed except for a home mortgage and always took a long-term perspective in her financial decision making.

We don't believe Aunt Avis's story is unusual. We don't have statistics, but we would guess that career single women do a better job of managing their finances than any other group in America today. They have no one else to depend on, so they seek good counsel and make sound decisions. Additionally, they don't have the major cash needs of a family.

This chapter will be the shortest in the book because the building blocks of financial success for a single woman can be found in the first five chapters plus chapter 17 (on investing). A career single needs to begin by learning and applying those principles. Then, after age thirty, only a few financial questions will come up; the balance of this chapter deals with them.

Should I Buy a House or Condominium?

The basis of this question is the common belief, dealt with in chapter 6, that not purchasing a home will leave you behind financially. The four assumptions that have made buying a home seem like the most attractive alternative are: (1) inflation; (2) low fixed interest rates; (3) deductibility of mortgage interest and property taxes; and (4) high income tax rates.

Purchasing a home on the expectation that it will appreciate in value assumes inflation. But home values don't always go up. In many areas of the country, they've gone down dramatically in recent years.

Low fixed interest rates are a thing of the past. Lenders have built into mortgage rates an inflation expectation that makes you, the borrower, pay for inflation.

The deductibility of mortgage interest and property taxes is now being attacked by Congress. High-income taxpayers have already lost a portion of that

If you're going to buy a home, it should be for reasons other than the economic benefits.

deductibility, and others may also. There's certainly no guarantee that home mortgage interest and property taxes will be forever deductible.

Additionally, tax rates are lower today than they've been in the past fifty years.

That means the tax benefit associated with mortgage interest and property taxes is less attractive today than ever before.

Career singles, then, shouldn't feel pressured to buy a home or condominium to provide financial security. Renting saves you a lot of cash that homeowners spend for maintenance, repairs, insurance, property taxes and so on. Investing those savings will give you the same financial security provided by appreciation in home values. In fact, you'll be more secure, because your savings *will* grow, whereas the owner's home may *not* appreciate in value. All this put together says that buying a home isn't required to provide financial security for anyone, let alone a career single.

Thus, if you're going to buy a home, it should be for reasons other than the economic benefits. Perhaps it provides some stability and roots you desire. In that case, it's a wise purchase rather than a good investment. It may turn out to be a good investment, but you shouldn't buy it with that expectation.

If you purchase a home, we offer the following suggestions regarding the financing. First, make a down payment of at least 20 percent. Second, choose a fixed rate mortgage rather than an adjustable. You can then plan for the future with certainty. Third, if you can afford to make the payments on a fifteen-year loan as opposed to the standard thirty-year loan, you'll have the mortgage paid off in half the time and with an enormous savings in interest expense.

Those aren't rules that will break you if you break them, but they're guidelines that will provide you with greater financial security sooner.

Do I Need a Will?

If you own property of any kind, you need to have a will prepared to ensure it will be distributed as you wish. The more assets you accumulate over the years, the greater the need for a will. Many times a career single, because she doesn't have the responsibilities of children, can do significant charitable giving through her estate plan, an approach we heartily endorse.

When you don't have a will prepared, you place the burden of distributing your property on someone else who may not understand your desires. So having a will prepared is not only good stewardship, but also a thoughtful act toward the person who will be your executor.

Do I Need Life Insurance?

Life insurance is usually bought to meet the needs of a surviving family. As a career single, you have no such needs to worry about. If you leave behind any debt, it can normally be repaid from the sale of assets you've also left, so there may not be a need for life insurance for that purpose, either.

Why, then, might you want to buy life insurance? Possible reasons include providing for the care of a parent or sibling; covering estate taxes; paying for your funeral expenses; and benefiting family, friends and charities. Here again, however, property in your estate could be sold to meet some of the needs, so life insurance may not be needed.

Your decisions about life insurance will depend on your desires and your estate size. All in all, life insurance needs for a career single are minimal. They should be considered carefully, however, before a decision is made.

Where Should I Invest My Retirement Funds?

Chapters 10 and 17 deal with investing in retirement and sequential investing, which are the same regardless of your marital status. Investment objectives in every case are income, appreciation, minimizing risk and maintaining some level of liquidity. It's impossible to find an investment that has no risk, total liquidity, continuous growth in value and generates a high yield. There are always trade-offs.

The only way to meet long-term goals with some degree of certainty is to diversify your investments among various classes of investment such as cash equivalents (like money market accounts), bonds, real estate, stocks and perhaps gold or silver. And the diversification needs to be done according to a strategy. A professional adviser can assist you in specific investment selection. Chapter 14 deals with how to pick an investment counselor, along with other types of advisers.

How Do I Decide How Much to Give?

One great benefit of not having a family to provide for is the opportunity to give at a higher level than someone else earning the same income. It may very well be that God has allowed you to remain single in part to be able to maximize your giving.

One of the great barriers to giving, however, is the fear of the future when you're the sole source of your financial security in retirement. For that reason, regardless of your income level, you should prepare a financial plan as outlined in chapter 4. It will help you determine whether you're on track to meet your long-term needs. If you are, maybe you can increase your giving merely by planning to do so rather than waiting until you reach retirement age.

You should consider three levels of giving. The "should give" level is the tithe amount discussed in various parts of this book. The "could give" level says that you choose to give money set aside for other purposes. The "would give" level comes from having prepared a financial plan and seeing God provide money in unexpected ways through either increased income or reduced expenses.

When you're operating from a financial plan, those unexpected increases in

*W*omen tend to make very good automobile decisions. In fact, they make better decisions than men.

cash are obvious and can be precommitted to giving. As a career single, you may have more opportunities to give than a married woman who, in many cases, has little control over the family finances.

How Do I Know What Car to Buy?

Buying cars was covered in chapter 5, and we recommend you read that section for a fuller treatment of the subject. But to summarize it here, the cheapest car you will ever own is the car you're presently driving. The longer you drive a car, the cheaper it becomes to operate. Whenever you buy a car, you should pay cash. If you can't afford to save for it, you can't afford to borrow for it. The time to purchase a different car is when the car has become unsafe or the cost, in terms of inconvenience for repairs, makes it uneconomical to continue repairing your current car.

Women tend to make very good automobile decisions. In fact, they make better decisions than men, because women are usually looking primarily for transportation, whereas men often let their egos get in the way.

Caring for Aging Parents

According to the *Financial Planning News* (Sept. 1990), "The task of caring for aging parents is more likely to fall to a single woman than to her married sister or her brother. Siblings assume that, because she is single and female, her life can more easily be arranged around the needs of Mom and Dad. And, being a good daughter, she usually agrees. Even if the others agree to help with their parents' care, the single woman still spends considerable sums on travel, groceries and incidentals that the parents mention they need. If she is the only child, the full economic burden falls exclusively to her."

A study commissioned by the U.S. House of Representatives in 1988 found that the average American woman will spend eighteen years helping aging parents.

Based on those facts, if your parents are still alive, you should probably plan on helping them at some point. You don't want such a major financial responsibility to take you by surprise. Perhaps the greatest potential need is to provide for catastrophic health care. Chapter 16 outlines some of the health insurance alternatives.

Conclusion

Being a career single may give you more opportunity for financial success than your married contemporaries have. You may also have greater opportunity to funnel the resources God has entrusted to you into the work of His kingdom.

Career singles generally do a better job of managing their money than any other group. That's to your credit. And you can probably enjoy greater certainty about your financial future than those women who have others that are dependent on them.

CHAPTER FOURTEEN

When and Where to Get Professional Advice

When asked what question she'd like to put to a prospective financial planner, a woman responding to our survey said, "Do you realize you hold my future in your hands?" Much does indeed depend on the quality of professional advice you receive. A story in the August 15, 1990, issue of the *Atlanta Journal & Constitution* portrayed what can happen when that counsel is bad. It told how Mabel Dixon of Cahokia, Illinois, lost her life savings when the savings-and-loan company in which she invested her money was taken over by the federal government and stopped paying interest on its notes. Ms. Dixon wept as she told her tragic story to a U.S. Senate committee in Chicago.

According to the article, "Ms. Dixon said that because she had to pay for expensive cancer treatments because she had no medical insurance, she was cautious about investing her money." Nevertheless, an official of the thrift had talked her into putting all her money into its unsecured debt offering.

Another victim of the same thrift, Marie Zarlingo, told the committee, "I trusted them because it was an old establishment. . . . It's really been a devastating thing."

This modern horror story raises the question, "If you can't trust your banker, whom can you trust?" Choosing a professional adviser, someone defined and licensed as an expert, can be extremely intimidating. You must face language barriers, fee barriers and confusion about where to seek advice for your particular situation. For example, do you need a CPA, a CFP, an LLB or a CFA? One woman raised a couple of common concerns when she told us, "All counselors seem to have their pet investments, and you never know how competent they really are." She concluded, "How do you know when you're getting good advice?"

That's a good question, because as Ms. Dixon and Ms. Zarlingo discovered, choosing the wrong adviser can be extremely costly. The fee paid is just one

The fee paid is just one expense associated with professional advisers. Bad advice can be far more costly.

expense associated with professional advisers. Bad advice can be far more costly. Ron recently visited with a person who was getting ready to declare bankruptcy. This man had been advising many couples in his church about investments and had lost more than $2.5 million of their money through poor decisions.

We've all heard sad stories about people who trusted advisers and got burned. But choosing qualified professionals should bring positive results for you. Good advisers can provide thorough legal documents, reduced taxes, prudent insurance plans and sound investment strategies.

Three questions typically come up in choosing professional advisers: When do you need them? What criteria do you use to evaluate them? And what process do you follow in choosing them?

When to Choose a Professional Adviser

There are many types of professional advisers, but the most common are lawyers, accountants, investment advisers, financial planners, insurance agents, real estate experts and bankers. Rarely will anyone need all of them. At times, however, you might need more than one.

Legal Advisers

We could write a full book on choosing a legal adviser, because there are so many specialty areas within the practice of law. At a minimum, you should seek legal advice any time you're dealing with lawsuits, divorce, estate documents, contracts or real estate transactions. Never practice do-it-yourself law; it may be less expensive in the short run but extremely costly in the long run. If you follow the process of choosing an adviser outlined in this chapter, you can avoid the pitfalls of picking poor legal advisers.

Accountants

Generally, two situations warrant help with your tax returns. One is if you've had any significant change in your financial situation during the tax year—for example, widowhood, divorce, a move or a capital gain transaction. The second is if your situation is complex because of owning a business, security transactions, caring for aging parents, large charitable contributions or other unusual itemized deductions. Occasionally we seek advice for particularly difficult questions. Because the tax laws are so complex and ever changing, even CPAs have trouble keeping up with them.

If you have a fairly simple return with routine itemized deductions, you probably don't need professional help.

Investment Advisers

Not until you reach step four of the sequential investment strategy and have at least $25,000 to invest should you need a personal investment adviser. Prior to that, you can get most answers from your own research.

Be aware that there is little regulation over who can and can't call themselves professional investment advisers. Virtually anyone can use the label. Because some people find the word *investment* mysterious or intriguing, many salespeople try to take advantage by calling themselves investment advisers. Even ordinary car purchases are sometimes called investments, which they are not.

Financial Planners

Having worked in the financial planning business for the last twelve years, Ron believes most people do not need a financial planner. What they need is a financial plan. He wrote the book *Master Your Money* to help people prepare their own financial plan without incurring the costs of a professional adviser.

As with investing, the financial planning industry is largely unregulated, and anyone can claim to be a professional adviser. Most so-called financial planners have no real training or expertise; they're really salespeople.

The critical difference between financial planners is how they're paid. Most get commissions for selling products and/or fees for services. Just a few are paid only a fee for their advice. We believe that fee-only financial planners are the only ones who can remain truly objective in giving advice, because they get no commissions from your investments or any insurance you buy. That doesn't guarantee the quality of their counsel, but it does make them objective, which is important.

If your income reaches $100,000 or you have more than $25,000 in investments, you may need a financial planner. Until then, however, you really just need a financial plan. If you require help preparing a budget or financial plan, read books on the subject and do it yourself, or contact your church to see if anyone in the congregation is qualified to help you.

Insurance Agents

It's wise to seek insurance counsel early on. Choosing the right products for your life, health, car and home is extremely important; it's also essential to being a good steward. Buying insurance is not a lack of faith but prudent planning in today's litigious society.

Banker

When America was more community centered, having a personal banker was a fact of life. Today, having a banker you can rely on is far less certain. Most banks are large, and branch managers are transferred regularly. You only need a relationship with a banker, however, if you require services other than checking, savings, credit cards, consumer loans and a safe deposit box. If you're going to invest using a bank (i.e., in CDs, money market accounts, etc.), you should find a banker in whom you have confidence—someone recommended by a satisfied customer whose judgment you trust, and someone who takes the time to explain everything clearly.

How to Choose a Professional Adviser

There are two keys to choosing good professional advisers. First, learn what criteria to use in evaluating and selecting them. Second, understand the process of making those choices.

Criteria to Use in Selecting

There are seven important criteria. The first four are "must" criteria. If the adviser you're interviewing doesn't meet any one of these, you should eliminate that person from consideration. The last three are important criteria, but they may not be essential. The criteria are as follows:

1. Technical expertise
2. Experience with similar clients
3. Wisdom and judgment
4. Likemindedness
5. Fees
6. Service
7. Location

The Selection Process

Three steps make up the selection process. Step one is to interview prospective advisers. Step two is to check their referrals. Step three is to have them send you an engagement letter.

During the initial interview, your goal is to see how well an adviser meets the seven criteria listed above by asking a series of questions.

To determine technical expertise, ask questions such as "What degrees have you earned? What type of training have you had relative to my particular situation? Have you ever been sued? If so, tell me the circumstances."

Those questions are not presumptuous, since you're going to pay for the person's services. The questions about being sued will indicate whether others considered this person to be competent. You could also ask if he or she has ever been used as an expert witness in a legal proceeding.

To check work experience, begin by asking, "Who are some other clients similar to me? What are some of the facts involved? What were the results in those situations?" You might also inquire about previous positions.

In discerning whether these advisers have wisdom and judgment, it would be good to know whom they rely on for advice. That would tell you whether they think they know it all or understand that gathering wisdom is a continuous process.

You might also ask, "Can you tell me about your family?" You're looking for the priority they place on their families. Professionals who spend a lot of time working and little time with family cut themselves off from the opportunity to gain wisdom from family, and that should concern you. Technical expertise is important, but you're looking just as much for judgment and wisdom.

In discerning likemindedness, your values and convictions should mesh as closely as possible with your advisers'. You should feel confident and trusting after your first meeting with each of them. Ask questions such as "What's the

Technical expertise is important, but you're looking just as much for judgment and wisdom.

biblical teaching on the issues we're discussing?" Ask about personal goals and why they chose to work in this field. Their answers will give you some idea of what motivates them. You are attempting to match the advisers' philosophies with your specific needs.

Everybody is concerned about fees charged by a professional adviser. Fees shouldn't be overemphasized, however. The four criteria above are more critical.

The greatest barrier to a satisfactory working relationship with an adviser is unrealistic expectations regarding fees. A professional, operating with integrity, is never concerned about discussing fees. Charges should be a reflection of the value of the service given and received. The problem comes when you start with improper expectations.

A balance needs to be struck regarding fees. Many times, paying too little will only get you lesser-quality service. On the other hand, paying too much is poor stewardship. But it's difficult for advisers to work with you if you continually balk at their normal fees, and you might find your work being lowered in priority. You want your advisers to receive a fair and clearly understood fee for services rendered.

Ron was recently involved in a minor accident in which a bicyclist was riding down the wrong side of the street and hit his car when he pulled away from a stop sign. There was no damage to the car, and the cyclist was only bruised. The father of the cyclist decided, however, to contact Ron's insurance company about a possible settlement.

Because it was in another state and Ron was uncertain of his own rights, he engaged an attorney in that state to assist him. When Ron asked about fees, he indicated they would be minimal. When Ron received his first bill for more than $1,000 and the process wasn't even half completed, he was extremely agitated. He hadn't pinned the lawyer down precisely enough on a fee quote. Of all people, Ron should have known better, but even he finds it difficult to ask about fees.

You need to ask three questions concerning fees: "How do you charge for your services? When do you bill? And what is either the range or the maximum fee for the services you'll perform for me?" Never enter into a professional relationship without knowing the answers to those questions.

It's also important to know how advisers will work with you. Creating realistic expectations is vital for a harmonious relationship. Ask potential advisers questions such as these:

How soon can I expect my telephone calls to be answered?

What is the projected turnaround time on this project?

How can I make your job easier and help you reduce the turnaround time?

How do you choose the staff assigned to my case?

Who will be doing the work specifically?

What are your goals in servicing clients? Do you always meet them?

When is the last time you lost a client? Why?

Do I really need you?

Another factor to consider is the location of your adviser. If frequent face-to-face meetings are needed, proximity is important. On the other hand, if most of your business can be conducted over the phone or with fax machines, even an out-of-town adviser can provide good service. Any concerns you have about proximity should be dealt with on the front end of the relationship.

After the interview process is completed, you're ready to check the references of those advisers in whom you're still interested. Talking to other clients about their experience with the advisers will give you peace of mind, knowing you've left no stone unturned.

When you've picked your advisers, you should ask them to send you an engagement letter you can sign and return spelling out several things: how your account will be serviced; the fees agreed upon; the length of the engagement. An ending point should be specified so you're not committing yourself to work with a given adviser perpetually, and the term should be no longer than one year. (At the end of that time, you can renew the agreement or not as you choose.) With this information on paper, you and the adviser are clear about expectations.

Last, a procedure for handling disputes needs to be outlined. Perhaps you'll agree to use mediation or a Christian conciliation service. Whatever the specifics, just realize disputes may come up, and you need to have predetermined how they will be resolved.

Conclusion

The process of choosing advisers may seem overwhelming, but remember the cost of picking the wrong ones. Time spent on the front end making good selections will save you dollars, frustration and time in the long run. Remember, too, that you're the employer; you're the one spending money for services. You're also the one who lives with the consequences of the advice taken. If the advisers you're evaluating don't have the patience to answer your questions now, they probably won't have the patience later to service you properly.

The good news is that you generally have more choices than time available to evaluate them all. Although there are lots of bad advisers out there, there are also many competent, trustworthy ones available to you.

In many ways, selecting a professional adviser is like choosing a marriage partner. There needs to be give and take, because not all aspects of the relationship will be smooth sailing. The more that's defined ahead of time, however, the greater the chances for a satisfactory partnership.

CHAPTER FIFTEEN

Life Insurance Do's and Don'ts

*D*r. Robert Witham was Judy's father. He completed medical school in the 1950s and became an anesthesiologist in Indianapolis, Indiana. He had absolutely everything going for him by the time he reached age forty. Successful in his chosen profession, he was doing well financially and had a happy family of one daughter and two young sons.

Judy's dad was typical of many people. He didn't trust life insurance agents, he really didn't understand all the terminology associated with insurance products, and he certainly didn't plan on dying in the foreseeable future.

Consequently, he avoided buying anything but minimal life insurance. Unfortunately, once he was diagnosed with incurable cancer at age forty-two, it was too late to purchase insurance. He lived only seven months after the cancer was discovered.

His life typifies what often happens in the life insurance arena. People are wary of salespeople, don't understand the terminology and certainly don't plan on dying anytime soon. As a result, people often experience what insurance agents euphemistically call "premature death"—one that occurs before a person either achieves financial independence or buys adequate life insurance.

For Christians, of course, there's no such thing as a premature death. Death may occur at an early age, but that doesn't make it premature in God's sight.

The Scriptures clearly indicate we can never be protected against death and all the changes it brings to a family. But the Scriptures are also clear that a husband is responsible to provide for his family (see, e.g., 1 Tim. 5:8). Very few families will ever achieve financial independence, however, so most will need life insurance as a cornerstone of an adequate financial plan. Let's look at some of the basic questions women often ask about life insurance.

What Should Life Insurance Provide For?

To make adequate provision for a surviving family, five needs must be covered. Those needs will vary over time, so your insurance ought to be reviewed periodically—at least every two years.

The first need is for income. Obviously, the death of the primary breadwinner creates a void. A young family has much greater needs than an empty-nest widow. At any point, however, a family will probably have some need for income.

A second need is to repay all borrowed monies. This may include debt from credit cards, mortgages, college education, investments or installment loans. Insurance should protect a family from being left with huge debts.

A third need is for major future expenses. For example, insurance might provide for children's college education. It might also cover the purchase of cars or a change in housing.

A fourth major need is for the emergency funds that will be required upon the death of the primary breadwinner—funeral expenses, legal and accounting expenses associated with the death and so on. We also suggest providing six months of living expenses in an emergency fund for the immediate and ongoing needs of the family.

Incidentally, if you depend on two incomes to meet your family's ongoing needs, life insurance should be bought to cover both earners. That's why we identify the income producer as the one who needs to be insured. It could be a man, a woman or both.

The last need that should be provided for is one most people don't consider, especially when they're young—estate taxes. Ironically, you don't usually need to worry about estate taxes unless you're adequately insured (*and* unless both spouses die in a common accident). When you're well insured, the large amount of proceeds may create an estate tax problem.

How Do You Determine the Amount of Coverage Needed?

When the primary wage earner dies, several things change financially. His or her income stops, some living expenses decrease, the tithe decreases, and pension plan contributions disappear. But some new income also *starts* flowing. For example, Social Security benefits are provided for a mother of young children and continue until the last child reaches college age. A widow will also receive Social Security benefits when she reaches retirement age. Additionally, there may be pension benefits from an employer, the military or a fraternal organization.

Once the facts are known about what income will stop, what income will start and the family's income needs, a decision can be made about how much life insurance to buy. For example, if you need to provide $20,000 of additional annual income upon the death of the primary breadwinner, a policy could be bought that would generate that amount.

The simplest way to determine the policy amount is to divide the income needed by an assumed earnings rate. For example, a need of $20,000 divided by an assumed earnings rate of 6 percent equals an investment fund needed of $333,333. If you had that amount in a bank account earning 6 percent interest, you would earn a total of $20,000 per year. (To be conservative, don't assume earnings greater than 6 percent.)

One consideration in determining the amount of income needed is whether or not the surviving spouse would continue working or go back to work. The answer will depend on the desire of you and your husband, the age of your children and the cost of insurance premiums. There's a trade-off between the desire not to work and the current life insurance premiums required to make that possible.

You should also consider your kids' insurance needs in the event of your own death. It's not pleasant to think about, but where would your children be if you and your husband were killed in an accident and you had been anticipating your work income to provide for them? Life insurance should be purchased on either you or your spouse to cover that contingency. Frankly, the more insurance you have on the primary breadwinner, the less pressure there is for the surviving family.

The income needed generally surprises people. One of the reasons insurance agents are often viewed with suspicion is that when they point out the needs, the

> *The more insurance you have on the primary breadwinner, the less pressure there is for the surviving family.*

potential purchaser is appalled at the figure and assumes the agent's self-interest is motivating that high projection. But usually the need *is* high, and the higher the income or life-style of the family, the greater the need for a large amount of life insurance.

Providing for Debt Repayment

Life insurance should provide for paying off all the family's debts, with the possible exception of the mortgage. (Preferably, however, it, too, would be paid off.) The total amount needed is easily determined by adding up the individual debts. To the extent that debts would be repaid, living expenses would go down, so the income replacement need outlined above would be less.

You may have heard of credit life insurance or mortgage insurance. Under those plans, monthly payments are simply added to your loan payment. This insurance is incredibly expensive, however; the same coverage can be bought much more cheaply through conventional life insurance.

Providing for College and Other Major Needs

The ages of your children will determine how much money will ultimately be needed to pay for college education. With college costs increasing at an average of 6 or 7 percent per year, the price doubles every ten to twelve years.

The best way to plan is to assume that death will occur tomorrow and your children will begin college immediately. If death did occur tomorrow and you had planned on a cost of $10,000 per year per child and had provided enough life insurance, you would have provided enough for the future years of college as well. That's because if the college fund were invested and growing at a rate of 6 to 7 percent per year, it would be increasing the same amount as college costs.

Generally speaking, life insurance should never be used as an investment vehicle to provide for college education. You may hear that you can save for college through life insurance while at the same time providing for the death of the breadwinner. That's true, but the type of insurance product that accumulates cash value will be far more expensive than other policies. The biggest consideration is not savings but provision.

Providing for Time

When someone dies, the survivors go through the shock of adjusting to life without that person. When the deceased was the primary breadwinner, the shock is not only emotional, but also financial. Many times the expenses associated with death and burial are large, especially if there was an extended illness and all the bills weren't covered by health insurance.

Before Judy's dad died, he received extensive and expensive treatment for cancer. He hadn't planned for that. Thus, a large part of his estate was eaten up by those bills, and the money to provide for his family's short-term and ongoing needs was greatly reduced.

In creating an emergency fund, figure on at least $10,000 to $15,000 for short-term medical and funeral expenses. Additionally, at least six months of living expenses should be provided. The exact amount will depend on your unique situation.

Providing for Estate Taxes

When you add together home equity, life insurance proceeds and company retirement benefits, it's not unusual for an estate to be much greater than anyone expected—large enough that estate taxes will be incurred.

Under current law, a person can leave any amount to a surviving spouse with no estate taxes. So the problem arises not upon the first earner's death but upon the surviving spouse's. When an estate goes over $600,000 in value from all sources, it will be taxed at very high rates unless it's left either to charity or a surviving spouse.

This chapter is not meant to cover how to plan for estate taxes but to warn you about the potential problem. (See Ron's book *Master Your Money* for more about estate planning.) Again, your estate plan, life insurance and wills should be reviewed at least every other year. At some point, you'll probably need professional advice.

If you accept the fact that you will die and calculate how much life insurance you need, you've answered the first big question concerning insurance. To pull your thinking together on the amount of coverage you need, the chart on the next page (fig. 15.1) summarizes the content of the previous paragraphs.

Figure 15.1

INSURANCE NEEDS ANALYSIS

Income goals for the family
  Living expenses (1)   _____
  Taxes   _____
  Giving   _____
  TOTAL INCOME NEEDED
                                               A

Sources of income (2)
  Social Security   _____
  Pension or retirement plans   _____
  Annuities or trusts   _____
Investment income (3)   _____
  Spouse working   _____
  Other   _____
  TOTAL INCOME AVAILABLE
                                              B

Additional income needed (per year) (4)
                                             B - A = C

Insurance required to provide income (5)
  (additional income needed x 10) (current need)
                                             C x 10 = D

Additional funds needed for:
  Funeral costs   _____
  Debt repayment (current need)   _____
  Estate tax and settlement expense (long-term need)   _____
  Education costs (current need)   _____
  Major purchases   _____

  _____   _____
  _____

TOTAL ADDITIONAL FUNDS NEEDED
                                              E

Insurance needed (6)
                                             E + D = F

Assets available for sale:
  Real estate   _____
  Stocks, bonds   _____
Savings available (to meet needs listed above) (7)   _____

  _____   _____

  _____   _____

  _____   _____

TOTAL FROM SALE OF ASSETS   _____
                                                        G

Total insurance needed (8)   _____
                                                        F - G = H

INSURANCE AVAILABLE NOW   _____
                                                        I

ADDITIONAL INSURANCE NEEDED   _____
                                                        H - I = K

NOTES

(1) Use 80% of present annual living expense.
(2) Income anticipated on a regular basis.
(3) Income from investments not liquidated.
(4) The total income needed less the total income available (B - A = C).
(5) This assumes the life insurance proceeds could be invested at 10% and provide the needed amounts. The investment percentage may be contingent on economic conditions or investment knowledge. The multiplication factor is 1 divided by the percentage return on insurance proceeds. Example: 10% = 1/.10 = 10; 8% = 1/.08 = 12.5; 12% = 1/.12 = 8.33. Thus, if you think you could earn only 8% from investing insurance proceeds, multiply the additional-income-needed figure by 12.5.
(6) Insurance needed is the sum of insurance to provide income (D) plus additional funds needed (E).
(7) Savings available would be only that part of savings that could be applied to meet the needs listed above. It would not include the savings needed to meet family living goals.
(8) Total insurance needed is the insurance needed less the amount available from the sale of assets (F - G = H).

Note: No adjustment has been made in these calculations for inflation. If you think you can earn 10% but that will be eroded by 3-4% inflation, you should use 6-7% in step 5 and not 10%. That will increase the amount of insurance needed. You can use any investment or inflation assumption you like.

What Kind of Insurance Should You Buy?

Bob and Laura met with George, who argued convincingly that they should cancel the life insurance they had purchased from a fraternity brother while Bob was in college. They should, George suggested, buy a much less expensive policy called term insurance from him and then invest the extra money in his company's mutual funds. George presented charts showing significant savings for them from this plan. Bob and Laura were extremely frustrated and confused, because this advice contradicted what they heard from Bob's fraternity brother many years before.

George was using terms like universal life, term life, whole life, decreasing term, increasing term, cash values, net asset values, front-end loads and commissions. Certainly his presentation was well intentioned, but his advice was confusing.

When they came to Ron, Bob and Laura asked, "What should we do?" The first thing Ron did was help them determine their life insurance need, approximately $500,000. They currently had $100,000 of coverage. There were a couple of other issues: whether or not to cancel the insurance they had and how they could ever afford $500,000 of life insurance. He advised them that the three questions they needed to answer were how much coverage they needed, how long they would need it and what they could afford.

The issue of how long you're going to need life insurance depends on whether you have a long-term financial plan in place. If you do, your insurance needs have already been determined. If you don't have a financial plan, you won't know when you've achieved financial independence (and so have no further need of life insurance) even if you do.

Bob and Laura had a financial plan in place that would provide for all their financial needs over the next twenty years assuming Bob continued to work and no unexpected needs arose. In the event of Bob's death today, however, they would need $500,000 of life insurance.

The rule of thumb is to not underestimate the growth in value of your estate when analyzing long-term life insurance needs. Chances are, Bob and Laura will continue to need $500,000 in coverage even after the children are gone and financial independence has been achieved. That's because their estate will continue to grow and the tax laws are likely to change over the next twenty to thirty years. Therefore, providing adequate insurance for the long term means buying more rather than less.

When most people reach age sixty or sixty-five, they find their life insurance needs do not disappear; rather, they're ongoing for different reasons. Also, many people who are overinsured at age sixty-five simply change the beneficiary of their insurance to a charitable organization and continue with the coverage.

What Type of Insurance Product Do I Need?

Before looking at specifics, we need to discuss how insurance works in general. Much of the confusion surrounding life insurance can be eliminated if you understand the basics.

All life insurance companies deal with the same three components: mortality costs, operating expenses and investment return. Each company is a business that takes the premium dollars received and invests them to achieve a return. The company then pays its operational expenses (personnel, underwriters, etc.) and the beneficiary proceeds when insured people die.

The company must do a good job of underwriting or the mortality costs may get out of control. If the company is lax when underwriting (e.g., allowing people who have cancer or heart problems to get insurance easily), its higher costs will be passed along to all policyholders.

The cash accumulation of an insurance company is the amount left after expenses and mortality costs are deducted from the income. (Depending on the type of insurance product, this cash accumulation may either be a dividend [in whole-life policies] or an accumulation side fund account [in universal-life products]. Universal-life policies don't have dividends per se.)

The cash accumulation eventually affects premium costs and/or rates of return on policies. Therefore, if the company wants to offer a low premium to attract new business, it can project high investment income and/or low expenses and mortality costs. The point is that it's next to impossible to be sure you're comparing apples to apples when examining insurance proposals, because it's difficult to determine if the proposals assume a "projected" or "historic" investment return, what mortality tables they're using, how accurately they project expenses and how well they control them.

Specific Type of Insurance

Insurance products come with many names, but there are really only four general types of life insurance policies. *Term policies* are purchased for a specific time period. *Whole-life policies* are purchased with the intention of maintaining them for an entire lifetime. (That's why whole-life insurance is sometimes called permanent insurance.) *Hybrid policies* combine both term and whole-life characteristics. *Universal life,* a relatively new product, is a hybrid investment-whole- life product.

Term insurance provides only death protection. If the covered person doesn't die within the policy period, the insured and his or her beneficiary get nothing from the company. The premiums depend totally on the age of the purchaser. The younger the purchaser, the lower the premiums; the older the purchaser, the higher the premiums. Term policies are prohibitively expensive for those over sixty years old, whereas for young people they're incredibly inexpensive—they can buy hundreds of thousands of dollars of coverage for only a few hundred dollars per year.

The premiums will increase greatly over time, however. That's why you have to know how long you're going to need life insurance. If you'll need it for a long time, you may want to consider the more traditional whole-life policy.

Whole-life policies offer a level amount of insurance, a fixed premium (it never increases) and a buildup of something called cash value, which is yours as the owner of the policy. That buildup, however, is nothing more than the return of premiums charged in excess of the risk taken by the company. They're called dividends, but they're not dividends in the traditional investment sense.

For those who have a long-term need for insurance, whole-life policies are less costly in the long run—when you total the premiums paid over a lifetime. But in the early years of a policy, the premiums are many times higher than the cost of the same amount of coverage in a term policy.

Without question, greater amounts of life insurance are needed when couples have young children. Almost any young couple can afford to be adequately insured with term insurance, and that's the route many of them will need to take. They may run out of affordable coverage at a later date, however, when they still have a need for life insurance, so permanent insurance should be bought when the budget allows.

Hybrid policies are combinations of whole-life and term policies, trying to get the best benefits from both types. The fixed premium is a benefit of whole life, but the lower premium is a benefit of term insurance. By mixing the amounts, a fixed premium can be set with a higher level of insurance purchased than with the traditional whole-life policy. These policies have many names, most designed to make the product more marketable.

The primary advantage of universal life is flexibility with regard to the death benefit and premiums. There's also flexibility in withdrawing cash from the policy. It is essentially a combination of an investment vehicle and term life insurance.

The main caution regarding universal life is that a company's earnings projections may or may not turn out to be true. The results depend on the economy, the performance of the company and how much you decide to invest in that particular product as time goes by. In general, we recommend avoiding universal-life products, because there are better investment and insurance alternatives.

Canceling Old Life Insurance Policies

You'll remember that Bob and Laura were also wondering whether to cancel the insurance they already had. They decided to do that and purchase a term policy, investing the difference in the monthly premiums.

That's a common recommendation of many life insurance companies. Some approach this recommendation ethically, and others do not. The primary concern is that you have adequate coverage. Also, you should have an insurance program you will maintain and not drop during a financial crunch. Whether or not to cancel old policies is not a simple problem; however, good policies with good com-

The best way to judge an insurance company is not by what it projects it will do but by its historical performance.

panies should usually not be canceled. (See the next section for how to evaluate companies.)

Although many consumer groups assert that permanent insurance is not a good buy, history has shown that companies that update and enhance their policies regularly are a viable investment alternative. Insurance should not be evaluated on the front end as an investment, but after a policy has been in force five to ten years, it must be looked at from a different perspective.

Many seven- to eight-year-old policies have a 6 to 9 percent tax-deferred return on the equity in the policy. Therefore, the argument that term is always better than whole-life policies misses two parts of the equation. First, there may be a long-term need for insurance that term cannot meet because it will eventually become too expensive. Second, existing whole-life policies may be a decent investment vehicle, especially considering the low risk and high liquidity they provide. Also, buying term and investing the difference implies that an individual is disciplined enough to invest the difference consistently, which is often not the case.

In summary, you need to evaluate your need for insurance with both a current and a long-term perspective. Current needs should probably be met in the least costly way, which would be term insurance. The long-term needs of flexibility and liquidity need to be met with a more permanent product when you can afford it.

Evaluating the Company behind the Product

To help you evaluate insurance companies, we offer the following guidelines:

Historical performance. The best way to judge an insurance company is not by what it projects it will do but by its historical performance. This is consistent with the philosophy of evaluating investment advisers, mutual funds and so on. How have they done in the past? How have their investments, expenses and mortality costs compared with those of other companies? How are they rated by *Best's Report?* (That's an independent rating service report; check in your local library.)

Look for a company that consistently has either met or exceeded what it projected. As a practical matter, because of the strong economy and inflation of the past three decades, all companies have exceeded their projections. So look at how a company has done compared to other companies and their own projections.

Treatment of old policies. A key question to ask an agent is whether the company updates its old block of policies to keep it current. In other words, is the company treating the old policyholders equitably with the new ones? If it doesn't give higher dividend yields to its old block of business to match the yields given to new policyholders, it is discriminating. It can also sell new products that way: "The policy I sold you a few years ago is outdated; here's a new one." (You want a company whose agents say, "We can update your old policy to be more in line with new products.")

In either case, such a company is not taking a long-term perspective. While you might get a good deal when you first buy a policy, in a few short years *you'll* be part of the old block of business, and then you may be the one discriminated against.

Most major mutual companies have updated or enhanced their old policies to bring them more in line with current policies. Those updates and enhancements take into account new mortality tables and higher investment returns. For the most part, stock companies have not done as well as mutual companies in updating their products. No stock companies are listed among the twenty companies in *Best's Report*.

A stock company is one owned by stockholders, with all the financial benefits going to them. A mutual company is one owned by the policyholders, with all the benefits going to them.

Portfolio versus new-money rates. Where an insurance company derives its investment return is another important consideration. One reason policies can meet projected returns and offer low premiums is that they've segregated money received recently (new money) from money that has already been received and invested (portfolio money, or money from premiums on older policies).

Insurance companies may have money they received in 1965 invested at 6 percent, money received in 1983 invested at 17 percent and money received in 1990 invested at 10 percent. When the whole portfolio is averaged, they may have a portfolio rate of 10 or 11 percent. That may be more or less than the rate of a company that's showing a new-money rate on premiums received recently. New-money products such as universal life typically must be invested short-term due to the flexibility they allow in premium payments.

For example, the projection used to illustrate a universal-life policy assumes a particular rate of return for the investment side of that product. Because the policy allows purchasers to withdraw money whenever they want, the company must always make short-term investments, not knowing when any group of policyholders might make withdrawals. Whole-life policies are sold as life insurance products, not investment products, so withdrawal of money is less likely to occur, and there may be a greater stability and rate of return.

Thus, you should select a company that will give a portfolio rate of return rather than a new-money rate because of the volatility of the latter. New-money rates of return are fine when interest rates are high, but when they're down, the portfolio rate will be much better. Here again, it's important to take a long-term perspective. The portfolio rate will be less volatile and provide more stability in your insurance program. Remember, you buy insurance first for protection, not as an investment.

In summary, you should choose insurance with a long-term perspective and not necessarily take the least expensive product. Historical investment return, portfolio rate versus new-money rates and company service should be taken into account as well. Service is more tied to the agent than to the company itself, so carefully evaluate the agent with whom you'll be dealing. The age of the company, its reputation and referrals from others are all important in determining whether the company will continue to provide the service you need.

If you have doubts about a company, contact the insurance commissioner of your state for additional information. Also, ask your agent to show you how the company is rated by the *Best's Report*. The December issue each year publishes actual performance histories of major companies. Finally, ask the agent to show you an in-force policy that's ten or more years old to compare with the current sales illustration.

Conclusion

Life insurance will never protect you or your husband against death, but it can provide for your family when it happens, which it certainly will at some point. How much coverage is needed is the first question to be answered, and then the secondary questions about cost and specific products can be more readily addressed.

Buying life insurance is similar to going to the dentist. You know you need to do it, but you certainly don't look forward to it. If you don't go to the dentist, however, you'll have long-term problems. If you don't evaluate your life insurance needs and purchase adequate coverage, you may not have long-term problems, but those who survive you probably will. Once again, it's important to remember that God has promised to provide wisdom to those who ask for it (see James 1:5). Ask Him for wisdom, do your homework, and then don't be afraid to make the necessary decisions.

CHAPTER SIXTEEN

*Health Insurance
Do's and Don'ts*

One of Ron's clients asked him to meet with her father, Dr. Shoaf. He had been a pastor all his life and had never earned more than $8,000 in any one year. Dr. Shoaf was eighty years old, and his wife, Margie, was eighty-one. They had enjoyed a long and fruitful marriage and ministry.

In the last year, Margie's health had deteriorated dramatically, and Dr. Shoaf had decided they needed to move to a long-term health-care facility. It was a complex where retired couples could rent or purchase apartments, and health-care needs were taken care of by on-site staff. If one of the residents required permanent hospital care, a nearby facility was available.

When Dr. and Mrs. Shoaf moved into the complex, their apartment cost about $10,000 per year. Now, however, because of Margie's deteriorating health, she was under full-time care, and their costs jumped to $40,000 a year. They asked Ron whether they could afford to stay in that facility.

God had blessed them with investments that had done very well, so they had enough resources to live out the rest of their lives, even at $40,000 per year. Ron was amazed that a man who had never made more than $8,000 a year was able to pay $40,000 a year to live and meet his wife's health- care needs.

Virtually everyone has been touched by the crisis in health insurance. Low-cost benefits once taken for granted by many Americans now have annual premium increases approaching 100 percent. For most of us, price increases usually come on discretionary items. When gasoline goes up, we carpool; when the price of beef increases, we eat chicken. Health insurance is different; we have to have it. A medical emergency could spell financial disaster.

Why is health insurance important in a book about women's finances? No one wants to face the risk of a catastrophic illness's depleting financial resources. Unlike auto insurance policies, health insurance policies' benefits and costs are difficult to understand and compare, which compounds the fear. This chapter will move systematically through the health insurance options and give guidelines for rational decision making. We are not helpless in controlling our costs.

Let's first look at where we've been, what health insurance is like now and what you can do about it.

In the 1960s and 1970s, American workers enjoyed increasingly comprehensive health-benefits packages from their employers. In addition to the basic medical plan for which most companies paid the entire premium, supplemental benefits were sequentially layered on top, such as dental and optical coverage. Some large plans even allowed certain elective benefits, such as cosmetic surgery.

The companies paid the premiums, the benefits were comprehensive, and expectations soon became conditioned for the medical plan to pay all the bills.

*W*e are not helpless in controlling our costs.

For many of us, any time we incurred an expense over twenty-five dollars, we checked our policies to see if it was covered.

Over the past three to five years, the pendulum has swung the other way. Not only are benefits no longer increasing, but they're even being curtailed. Most individuals can't look to their major medical plans to provide free, comprehensive benefits anymore.

Two reasons exist for this accelerating shift. First, health benefits were abused. Individuals were reimbursed for every conceivable illness or procedure, and a minority of unscrupulous doctors grew rich billing inflated charges to both the government and private insurance companies. If receiving a reimbursement on your medical insurance takes longer today than it did five years ago, it's because insurance companies make certain fraud is not occurring.

Second, with the advances in medical technology, the cost of treatment has also increased. Diagnostic procedures such as a simple x-ray have evolved into a magnetic resonance image (MRI) that can cost up to $1,000 per procedure. We get much better care—but also higher costs. Even when less expensive tests will suffice to diagnose an illness, many doctors, fearful of malpractice suits, will order the more-expensive and comprehensive tests.

Where Are We Now?

As health insurance premiums became a larger percentage of employee compensation, employers were forced to take a hard look at this benefit. Many companies that used to pay all employee and dependent coverage now ask employees to bear part or all the cost for dependents. Many employers are also asking employees to pay a percentage of their individual coverage. The theory is that as employees begin to bear some of the cost, they will become intelligent consumers of medical services and have a personal interest in holding down expenses.

A third way employers are saving is by reducing the benefits available. Many plans are eliminating the hard-to-diagnose illnesses, such as psychiatric care. Insurance companies are also raising the deductibles, the portion the employee pays prior to the insurance's "kicking in."

In summary, individuals are being asked to bear more responsibility for their own health care and can no longer expect the types of benefits they enjoyed in the past. Those who take care of their health and can bear the risk of paying some of their own medical expenses will be rewarded with significantly reduced health insurance costs.

Health Insurance Terminology

Shopping for health insurance is an unpleasant chore. Unlike many products we buy that can easily be compared to one another, medical insurance policies are written in unfamiliar language and are usually dissimilar to one another. The challenge is to compare the costs versus the benefits you will receive and match the policy to your specific economic situation. The four main terms used in medical insurance policies are:

Deductibles. The deductible is the amount of money an insurance company requires the policyholder to pay before benefits are paid. Minor illnesses requiring a routine doctor's office visit are rarely covered because of the deductible clause. Most policies used to have a $100 deductible, but a $500 deductible is becoming increasingly common. If you have a $5,000 medical treatment and your policy calls for a $500 deductible, you'll pay the first $500 of this claim before benefits begin.

Co-insurance. This is usually the percentage amount you pay on any procedure the company considers eligible. Most major-medical policies pay 80 percent of eligible expenses. In the $5,000 example above, after you satisfy the $500 deductible, the insurance company would pay 80 percent of the remaining $4,500, or $3,600. You would be responsible for 20 percent, or $900. Your out-of-pocket costs so far are thus $1,400.

Out-of-pocket or stop-loss maximum. Insurance companies realize that with catastrophic illnesses like cancer, medical bills can run in the hundreds of thousands of dollars and would put an unrealistic co-insurance burden on most families. Thus, most policies contain a co-insurance maximum or stop-loss clause. To illustrate, let's assume you had a new $10,000 medical expense and a policy with a $1,000 co-insurance maximum. Since you had already satisfied your deductible for this year and paid $900 in co-insurance (see above), you would be responsible for only $100 of this new bill.

Lifetime maximums. Most major-medical policies have lifetime maximum benefits they will pay, usually $1 million to $2 million. A few have no lifetime cap. When selecting a policy, make sure the lifetime cap is at least $1 million so that a catastrophic illness or accident won't wipe you out financially.

How to Compare?

The bad news is that today's medical insurance policies are expensive and complicated. The good news is that for those willing to take the time to educate themselves and effectively compare policies, premium dollars can be saved. Many policies and employers allow you to tailor your medical coverage to your individual needs.

People who have a high net worth and relatively good liquidity may choose a medical policy with an extremely high deductible in exchange for low monthly premiums. For someone with several hundred thousand dollars in the bank, an expense of a few thousand dollars is not the catastrophic blow it would be to someone with only several hundred dollars.

A single parent on a budget could actually need more coverage than a multi-millionaire. One person can obviously afford to take more risk than another, yet both individuals probably need the same lifetime cap, since a catastrophic illness would be equally devastating to either individual. You might also be able to select a different co-insurance percentage to coincide with your financial circumstances.

For example, one person might want the insurance company to pay 80 percent of all medical charges after the deductible is satisfied, with a maximum per-

*Y*ou should only insure yourself against events that would have a catastrophic impact on your life.

sonal liability of $2,000 per year. A more wealthy individual might choose a 30 percent co-insurance figure with a $10,000 stop loss. Many people who manage their finances prudently can afford to bear some of the medical risk cost themselves and pay lower insurance premiums as a result.

A general rule of thumb is that most people can afford to bear *small* risks more efficiently than paying the insurance company to cover them. Those companies obviously have to pay for their overhead and make a profit, and that drives up your premiums. A second rule of thumb is that you should only insure yourself against events that would have a catastrophic impact on your life. If eye care insurance, for example, costs too much for the benefit received, drop it.

Further Note on Deductibles

Most Americans spend 5 to 15 percent of their annual income just to protect themselves with life, homeowners, automobile and medical insurance. Simultaneously increasing your deductible on your car, homeowners and health insurance policies can save several hundred, if not thousand, dollars in annual premiums.

Remember, deductibles are calculated on a calendar term. The probability of accidents occurring in all three areas—home, auto and health—in one year is slim. If you raise the deductibles in all three areas, the savings in premiums each year will more than likely offset any increased out-of-pocket costs from claims.

Action Step: Contact your insurance carriers, and find out how much you can save by increasing your deductibles. Place your premium savings in a separate savings account for that rainy day when you have a claim. If you never have a claim, you'll be far ahead.

What Kind of Policy Should You Buy?

Insurance rates and laws differ from state to state, and it would be beyond the scope of this book to give specific recommendations. The following advice is meant to be general, but it does provide a systematic method for choosing health insurance.

Employer-Provided Policies

For most people, the best medical insurance can be obtained through their employer. Usually, the larger the company, the less expensive the premium and the greater the benefits offered. Insurers like working with relatively large, homogeneous groups, and the larger the number of workers covered under any one policy, the more efficiently a company can administer and deliver basic coverage. That doesn't mean group coverage is always less expensive, but it almost always offers better predictability of coverage and premium charges. Your human resources or benefits department will shop the market for the best policies available.

Even if you quit your job, you may have the right to continue your present coverage for at least eighteen months under the federal government's COBRA law. COBRA was enacted to prevent high-risk or uninsurable, terminated employees from being left without medical benefits. The premiums may be slightly higher, and benefits may not always equal what your employer offered, but you're still considered to be in a group even though you no longer work for the employer.

Women who are facing a divorce may lose their husbands' health benefits. Care should be taken in drawing up the divorce agreement to ensure the children are still covered under the employer's plan and that any alimony payments will take into account the high cost of finding an individual policy for the divorced spouse.

Individual Policies

When shopping for private policies, individuals can choose from two categories: major medical or hospital-surgical. Major medical is the most comprehensive, usually paying for outpatient care. It is the most similar to employer-provided plans.

Hospital-surgical policies usually cover only in-hospital services and surgical procedures. Because these policies don't offer first-dollar coverage, they're considerably less expensive than major-medical policies. First-dollar coverage means the insurance company begins paying with the first dollars you spend. Major-medical policies, on the other hand, typically begin paying *after* you pay your deductible. Hospital-surgical policies should not be eliminated as an alternative, because they cover the huge, catastrophic bills. If you have a large net worth, this policy may provide you with the best trade-off between costs and benefits.

Where do you shop for individual policies? Here are a few suggestions:

Blue Cross, Blue Shield. Your first stop should be your local Blue Cross, Blue Shield office. Traditionally, Blue Cross has been the best provider of insurance for those ineligible for group coverage. A note of caution, however: There is a great disparity between states on the quality of coverage. Be sure to investigate carefully.

Group associations. Small employers can often obtain the benefits of larger group plans through trade associations. For example, we know of one person who was able to join the local chamber of commerce and obtain a far better policy than he could have on his own. When you own a small business, even with only one or two employees, it may profit you to pay some annual dues in order to receive group discounts on health or disability insurance.

Private carriers. If you're healthy and have no pre-existing medical problems, you might be able to find an individual insurance policy that can be tailored to your financial situation and even offer reasonable premiums.

Be advised that not all salespeople are experts in all areas of insurance. The health-care industry, like other areas of business, has become highly specialized. Just because someone wants to sell you a policy, do not assume the person can provide you with the *best* policy for your situation.

How do you find an agent? First, ask for referrals. Find someone who has had a claim, and see if his or her agent was helpful. Second, ask an agent what percentage of his or her annual income comes from the sale of health-insurance policies. As a rule of thumb, don't buy a policy from anyone who doesn't make at least one third of his or her income from the sale of such policies.

Health maintenance organizations (HMOs). The insurance alternatives mentioned so far are traditional in the sense that people have the freedom to get treatment from the doctors and other professionals of their choice. But HMOs limit that freedom in exchange for lower monthly premiums or expanded coverage; they become the actual providers of medical services.

An individual or family joins an HMO, which runs its own clinic(s). If you have an illness, you go there and receive care from a staff doctor. There's no guarantee you'll see the same doctor twice, so you give up the usual doctor-patient relationship.

These organizations offer several advantages, however. First, many expenses not covered under most traditional health plans, such as routine checkups, are provided for in an HMO. Second, since an HMO does the administrative work usually performed by an insurance company, there are no complicated forms to complete when you go; usually, you just show your membership card.

If cost is your primary consideration in choosing health insurance, HMOs are worth looking into. You'll find them listed in the Yellow Pages of the phone book. Compare costs and services carefully relative to those in traditional plans.

A word of caution: a few HMOs have gone bankrupt or left certain localities recently. So before enrolling in one, check with your state insurance commissioner to make sure that HMOs that go out of business are required to offer conversion plans with other insurance carriers. To be extra safe, consider only those HMOs that have been operating in your state for at least ten years and have a good record with the insurance commissioner.

Preferred provider plans (PPPs). Another nontraditional form of health insurance is the PPP. In these plans, an insurance company contracts with a number of local doctors to provide services at fees that are normally discounted from their standard fee schedules. Thus, individuals have some choice in which doctor they see, and they can go back to the same doctor, but the choice is limited to those doctors who are in the plan, especially in certain instances such as when major surgery is needed.

Companies that offer these plans usually offer traditional insurance as well, so if you have a traditional plan now, you might ask your agent if a lower cost PPP is available. Employers often give their employees incentives, such as smaller deductibles, to use PPPs.

In summary, when buying medical insurance, you'll often be torn between conflicting objectives: lower cost versus the traditional freedom of choosing your own doctors, dentists and so on. But if cost is your overriding concern, HMOs and PPPs should be considered seriously.

Other Types of Insurance

Supplemental Health Insurance

Supplemental coverage includes policies limited to specific illnesses, such as cancer. Usually these policies are offered by little-known companies that specialize in such coverage. Because cancer is one of the diseases we fear most and the annual premiums of $300-$500 are relatively low, these policies are often an easy sale, especially as people grow older. Are they a good buy? Generally not.

If you're willing to pay an extra $500 per year for a cancer policy, you would be better off using that additional premium to beef up your major medical policy.

Nursing Home Insurance or Long-Term Health-Care Policies

Policies that protect you from catastrophic, long-term nursing home expenses are relatively new and are often sold on a fear basis, as everyone reads about projected Medicare cuts. The discussion of such policies forces individuals to answer the unpleasant question "Who will take care of me when I'm old?"

An adequate discussion of these policies is beyond the scope of this book. But as the public becomes more aware of them, they should become a reasonable insurance alternative. Prices will go down, and benefits will be increased. Be sure you're an informed consumer when considering these policies, however, as the "fine print" is far more detailed than in most medical policies.

Before considering one of these policies, discuss your long-term care concerns with loved ones and family. A plan that has the agreement and wisdom of multiple generations is far better than one decided upon by the grandparents alone.

Second, do not buy a policy out of fear. That's usually how they're sold, and most purchases based on fear are made unwisely. Many policies eventually lapse because of high premiums.

Third, purchase these policies only from a company you know.

Ask the agent for reports on its financial strength, age, size, history, reputation and cash reserves. If you have questions about the financial strength of the company, get counsel from an adviser you trust.

Good News for Christians

Just as Christians are called to be different in their behavior, so also they can approach the health-insurance area with confidence instead of despair. In 1963, Dr. S.E. McMillen wrote a book titled *None of These Diseases*. It focuses on the Bible's practical directives to save one from certain infectious diseases, cancers and psychosomatic illnesses. Obviously, prevention is better than any medical insurance policy. We highly recommend the book.

Considerable research attributes many forms of cancer to stress. The Christian has a stress reliever in Philippians 4:6, which says, "Do not be anxious about anything . . ." A healthy spiritual relationship can prevent the onset of many diseases.

Christians should be able to bear more of their medical risk themselves than the U.S. population as a whole. In general, Christians do not smoke or drink, or they do so moderately. If you take care of your health and come from a family without a history of medical problems, you're a good candidate to take higher deductibles and co-insurance and pay lower premiums.

Remember, when you buy a group policy, rates are established by including you with a certain percentage of smokers, closet alcoholics and so on. In other words, insurance companies pool good risks with the bad ones. If you are healthy, your likelihood of making a claim is less than that of the overall population, and you should pay accordingly.

Finally, when buying medical insurance, don't do so out of fear. Everyone should have a basic plan, but as with anything else, health insurance can be carried to an extreme. When making the difficult decisions, God has given us a sound mind: "For God did not give us a spirit of timidity, but a spirit of power, of love and of self-discipline [or sound judgment]" (2 Tim. 1:7). We should be able to make good decisions based on the assurance that our future is in the hands of our heavenly Father. We should be less susceptible to the fear-based marketing tactics often used.

In summary, even in an area with costs that are skyrocketing, you can save money by understanding that the market is changing, purchasing coverage that makes sense for your financial situation, raising your deductibles, maintaining a healthy relationship with the Lord and taking care of yourself physically.

CHAPTER SEVENTEEN

Getting Ahead Step by Step

*M*ary Alice approached Ron just prior to a speaking engagement in Houston. She complimented him on the books he had written, told him she had inherited a lot of money and married a wealthy man in east Texas, and then made a startling statement.

"You know," she said, "no one ever told us to spend less than we earn." Mary Alice and her husband were surrounded by professional advisers and had themselves been successful financially, yet no one had told them that the key to longterm financial success is to spend less than you earn.

Everything we have talked about in this book should be encouraging you to create a positive cash flow by spending less than you earn. While you're doing that, you should be making decisions to provide adequate insurance and solve problems that have arisen, and you should be making wise choices about buying a home, cars and furniture, providing for children's educations and so on.

When you spend less than you earn, you'll have money that needs to be invested, saved or whatever else you want to call it. Where to put that excess cash flow is a question transcending the financial seasons of life.

You're bombarded by investment alternatives every day. One of the worst causes of confusion is that many things are called investments that aren't. For example, cars, houses, exercise machines, self-development programs and so forth are not really investments. An investment is a purchase you make expecting that it will provide an income or be sold for a higher price later, when it appreciates in value. Cars, homes and exercise machines may be wise purchases, but they're not usually investments.

It's true that homes have increased in value consistently over the last thirty to forty years. But as we pointed out earlier, a home is not bought as an investment. It's purchased to provide a place to live, and it happens in many cases to turn out to be a good purchase.

A chapter on investing is a fitting conclusion to this book for several reasons. First, as mentioned earlier, investment questions transcend financial seasons of

We don't plan because we lack faith; rather, by faith we plan, realizing God will meet our needs regularly.

life. Second, following the plan in this book should provide the resources to invest. Third, saving, planning and investing for the future are all critical elements in achieving ultimate financial success. Losing money through foolish investments is tragic and unnecessary.

We read in Proverbs 21:31, "The horse is made ready for the day of battle, but victory rests with the Lord." That verse summarizes well the combination of prudent planning and faith. We plan carefully for the future, but we realize that ultimate victory and protection come only through our Lord. We don't plan because we lack faith; rather, by faith we plan, realizing God will meet our needs regularly.

Sequential Investing

Throughout this book we have talked about sequential investing, which is nothing more than investing according to a step-by-step plan. Just as you climb a set of stairs one step at a time, so investments need to be made one step at a time.

Figure 17.1

SEQUENTIAL INVESTING

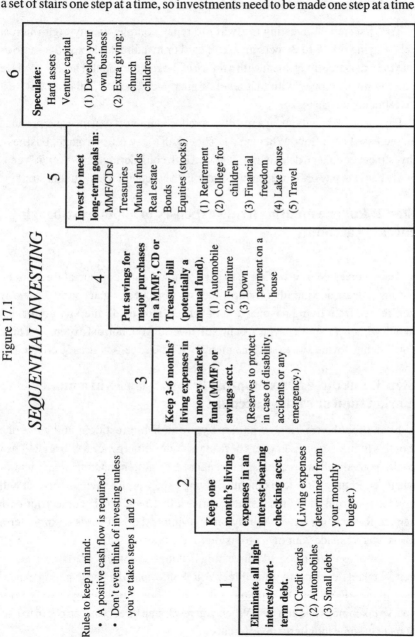

Rules to keep in mind:
- A positive cash flow is required.
- Don't even think of investing unless you've taken steps 1 and 2

1

Eliminate all high-interest/short-term debt.

(1) Credit cards
(2) Automobiles
(3) Small debt

2

Keep one month's living expenses in an interest-bearing checking acct.

(Living expenses determined from your monthly budget.)

3

Keep 3-6 months' living expenses in a money market fund (MMF) or savings acct.

(Reserves to protect in case of disability, accidents or any emergency.)

4

Put savings for major purchases in a MMF, CD or Treasury bill (potentially a mutual fund).

(1) Automobile
(2) Furniture
(3) Down payment on a house

5

Invest to meet long-term goals in:

MMF/CDs/
Treasuries
Mutual funds
Real estate
Bonds
Equities (stocks)

(1) Retirement
(2) College for children
(3) Financial freedom
(4) Lake house
(5) Travel

6

Speculate:
Hard assets
Venture capital

(1) Develop your own business
(2) Extra giving: church children

Step 1: Pay off high-interest debt

The first step in investing is always to repay completely any high-interest debt. Paying off 18 to 21 percent credit card or installment debt is the same as making a risk-free investment with a return of the same amount. There is no place you can invest money with that level of guaranteed return. This is the wisest investment you can make.

Paying off debt will always result in a reduced interest expense and produce an increased cash flow. Whether you should also pay off mortgage, business, investment or college debt at this stage is worth considering. However, it's generally better to pay off mortgage debt later in the sequential investment strategy.

Step 2: Put one month's living expenses in an interest-bearing checking account

The second step of investing is to give yourself a little financial freedom by putting at least one month's living expenses in a checking account. That way you're free from living paycheck to paycheck. You could literally go for one month without having a paycheck and still meet all your normal expenses. Think how freeing it would be to start the month with the expenses already covered!

Step 3: Put three to six months' living expenses in a money market fund or savings account

Even though you've now paid off your high-interest debt and have one month's living expenses in your checking account, emergencies will arise. They could be medical emergencies, car repairs, a forgotten insurance payment or whatever. Putting three to six months' living expenses in a savings account will protect you from such unpleasant surprises. In effect, you become your own banker. Rather than having to rely on high-interest credit cards or short-term loans, you've made your own provision for the unexpected.

You shouldn't even consider investing in things like stocks or real estate until you've taken steps one, two and three. You should consider participating in pension plans, IRAs, KEOGH plans or 401-Ks from your employer only after you've taken steps one and two. When you reach step three, you can begin to participate in some long-term investments.

Step 4: Save for major purchases

Once again, we recommend that you become your own banker by planning ahead for automobile purchases, home down payments, future vacations and other major purchases. It's always better to have interest working *for* you rather than *against* you. When you save for major purchases, you're not only saving what you don't spend, but you're also accumulating more through the magic of compounding. It's *always* better to be a lender than a borrower.

Where do you park the money being saved for steps three and four? Listed below are several options that maintain a high degree of liquidity and safety, yet maximize your investment returns.

1. Checking accounts. Most banks offer interest-paying checking accounts at passbook savings rates (NOW accounts) provided a stipulated minimum balance is maintained. In some cases, free checks may be included. If you keep one month's living expenses in checking, you'll probably qualify for these accounts. But beware: In some areas, monthly service charges can be large.

2. Passbook savings accounts. These accounts are available at any bank or savings and loan. The interest rates paid are usually low unless you can meet certain minimums to qualify for higher rates.

3. Market investment accounts. These savings accounts at local banks pay money market rates (usually higher than the passbook savings rate). Different banks give them different labels. Ask for their money market account. These usually require a minimum balance (e.g., $1,000) and limit you to three checks per month.

4. Credit unions. Credit unions usually offer slightly higher interest rates than banks on both checking and savings accounts. During times of low interest, they may even beat the money market funds. They also have the advantage of offering direct deposit for your paychecks.

5. Money market funds (also called money market mutual funds or daily money funds). These funds generate money by making short-term loans. The rates vary daily according to the prevailing market interest rates. If rates increase, money market funds will track this rise. If rates fall, the funds will track downward. The funds are as liquid as checking accounts, and most offer check-writing privileges. Money market funds are good parking places for short-term funds or funds being accumulated for investment.

Since money market funds are not federally guaranteed and may not be insured, you should read the offering prospectus carefully before investing. It's reassuring to know, however, that no one has ever lost money in a money market fund.

6. Certificates of deposit (CDs). These are savings certificates in which you invest for a specified time, anywhere from a month to several years. Some banks or credit unions may offer a percentage point or two premium in exchange for your willingness to tie up your money for a guaranteed period. These CDs can be a good place to park money as long as you don't commit it for more than one year. If an emergency arises, you can either make a premature withdrawal or borrow from the bank using the CD as collateral.

Many people seeking investment advice are not really in a position to invest because they haven't met basic priorities. Notice that the structure of the sequential investment strategy is geared toward making and keeping you free of debt. It follows the philosophy that you should save before you buy. That may be old-fashioned, but it works!

Before going on to steps five and six, you need to understand the difference between tools, techniques and vehicles. Specific investment *vehicles* include stocks, bonds, T-bills, gold, silver, land, mutual funds, real estate and so on. One popular *tool* for investing in those specific products is an IRA, which is basically the same as a pension plan. Dollar-cost averaging (committing a fixed amount of money per month to a particular investment, resulting in a low per-unit cost) is a *technique* of investing. Market timing is another technique that results, one hopes, in selling near the top of the market and buying near the bottom.

Each tool and technique uses one of the specific investment vehicles to accomplish its objective. For example, you might establish an IRA (the tool) to save for retirement, putting your money into stocks (the vehicle) by investing a set amount in a mutual fund each month (the technique known as dollar-cost averaging). The techniques require a great deal of expertise to be effective and should be used only with the assistance of a professional. The tools require merely that you know whether a particular tool fits your situation and then how to implement it using one of the vehicles. The tools and techniques can be used during either the accumulation or the preservation phase of investing.

Step 5: Invest to achieve long-term goals

It's important to remember you still are not financially independent when you begin to accumulate money for long-term goals. Most people won't get beyond step four, even if they've done a good job of financial planning and money management. But even if you do, you still have not met the long-term goals of retirement, college education, getting out of mortgage debt and so on. Thus, you still can't afford to invest in places that put you at risk of losing your money. Many investments are purely speculative in nature, and while they promise high rates of return, they come with a corresponding level of risk.

Thus, the investment vehicles you use to meet your long-term goals should not be too risky. Concern for minimizing risk, however, tends to make people *overly* cautious in their investment strategy, especially as they approach retirement. Therefore, in the next few pages we'll try to remove some of the uncertainty about investing. This is not meant to be a complete description of how to achieve investment success, but when it's used prayerfully to make investment decisions, it should help.

The Investment World, Past and Future

In 1980, the three biggest financial concerns a family faced were inflation, taxes and high interest rates. Inflation was running in the double digits, taxes were as high as 70 percent, and interest rates on home mortgages were at 13.16 percent in July. The best investment over the previous five years had been gold, which returned a 254 percent gain over that period, even after taxes. The Dow Jones Industrial Average on July 21, 1980, was at 923.

The predictions for the 1980s by almost everyone said inflation would continue to increase, perhaps even approaching triple-digit levels by mid-decade. By 1985, forecasters said, we were almost certain to have some type of economic crash or depression, and by 1990 the dollar was projected to be worthless.

In reality, inflation dropped back to below 5 percent per year, taxes were reduced to the lowest rates in over fifty years, and interest rates came back down to late-1960 levels. Between 1980 and 1989, we had the longest period of economic growth in our country's history. The dollar did depreciate in value, but it certainly did not become worthless. At the end of 1989, more money from outside the U.S. was flowing into this country than any other country in the world, which demonstrated a strong faith in our economy.

If you look at what happened in the investment world during the 1980s, however, you discover that every area crashed at least once. The stock market experienced the crash of 1987, bond prices crashed in the early 1980s, farmland values collapsed, gold has been one of the worst-performing investments for the decade, silver crashed, numismatic coins performed poorly, art and collectibles did not appreciate well, real estate in various parts of the country experienced tremendous crashes, and so on. That's not to say that any of those were bad investments over the entire ten-year period. But at some point during those years, every investment class crashed at least once.

There are plenty of predictions about what's going to happen by the year 2000. The biggest concerns seem to be the federal budget deficit, the balance-of-payments deficit, increasing consumer debt, the decreasing savings level and high housing prices. In other words, as we look to the years ahead, we find tremendous uncertainty, confusion and fear (just as in 1980). No one, however, can predict the next year—let alone ten years—with any certainty. People can only make educated guesses, and those guesses are wrong more often than not.

In light of that uncertainty, how do you preserve your investments? If you make an investment of $1,000, will it still be worth $1,000 when you cash it in?

No one can predict the next year—let alone ten years—with any certainty.

If you deposit it in a bank savings account, fifteen years later you can withdraw that same $1,000 plus whatever interest it has accumulated. That's presumed to be the safest type of investment. However, if we've had inflation of 5 percent per year over that same period, the $1,000 saved is worth only $481 in purchasing power. That's called the inflation risk. Most long-term, income-producing investments, such as savings accounts, Treasury bills, CDs and bonds, face that risk.

They also face an interest-rate risk. For example, if you invest in a bond and interest rates rise, your bond will be worth less than its original purchase price.

The lower the coupon rate and longer the term of the bond, the greater the decline in value as interest rates rise. (That's because other investors can get a better rate on new bonds, so they're not going to pay full price for your old bond; they'll pay an amount that effectively makes your bond pay the same rate as a new bond.) On the other hand, of course, if interest rates decline, bond values rise.

Most investors assume that bonds, Treasury bills, cash, savings accounts and other fixed-rate vehicles are the safest type of investment to make. But the truth

---

*M*aintaining a long-term perspective is critical for investment success.

---

is that during times of rising interest rates or inflation, they're the riskiest investments you can have. During those times, generally speaking, the stock market, real estate, perhaps gold and other investments that are variable day to day will do better.

Market-type investments have two risks of their own, however. One is a market risk—they can lose value due solely to a decline in investor confidence. Rising interest rates or poor economic conditions may make investors anxious and unwilling to buy investments except at reduced prices, even though there has been no real change in the underlying assets.

There's also a very real economic risk associated with variable types of investments. For example, real estate values tend to decline when overall economic conditions are bad in an area. When people are out of work, they don't buy houses. The stock of a company will go down, not up, if it loses money rather than making a profit, especially if investors expected it to do better.

Where do you invest if every investment has risks? Four keys lead to good decisions; they won't eliminate the risk, but they'll balance risk so overall investment returns can be positive.

Keys to Investment Success

Long-term perspective. We may sound like a broken record by now, but maintaining a long-term perspective is critical for investment success. If you've established an investment strategy prior to retirement, retiring should not change that strategy. Your life expectancy at age sixty-five is more than twenty years, and twenty years is too long to maintain a short-term perspective.

If you had invested $10,000 in the stock market in 1970 and left it there until the end of 1989, with your stocks doing as well as the Dow Jones Industrial Average, you would have experienced an average annual return of 12.8 percent. Your $10,000 would have grown in value to $87,900, or almost a ninefold increase.

However, had you retired in 1970 and put all your money in passbook savings accounts to avoid losing any of it, twenty years later you would indeed have your $10,000. But even if you left the income in the passbook account to be reinvested, the $10,000 would at best have grown to something under $25,000—less than a third of the $87,900.

How do you know when to invest in the stock market, real estate, gold or any other market? You don't. No one knows when the market will reach the bottom or top. If you try to buy low and sell high, you're more apt to buy high and sell low. That's true even for professional managers. It has been proved that no one can consistently know when to buy low and sell high. The only sure way to invest is to take a long-term perspective, understanding that investment values will go through cycles. At some point they'll be up, at another they'll be down, but the overall trend is upward.

Another illustration of the value of a long-term perspective is stock market investments over ten-year periods. Suppose that every year beginning in 1900, you bought all stocks included in the Dow Jones Industrial Average and held them for ten years. Then, in the eleventh year, you sold the stocks bought ten years earlier, and you did this same thing year after year. There was only one ten-year period from 1911 through 1989 when you would have suffered a loss on your portfolio.

That strategy doesn't require expertise, just a long-term perspective on investing. The problem is, most people insist on trying to buy low and sell high rather than taking the conservative approach of buying and holding over a long term.

Diversify. You have no doubt heard that the key to real estate investing is location, location, location. That's true. Similarly, one key to investing is diversify, diversify, diversify.

You can diversify three ways. The first is by asset class, such as stocks, bonds, real estate, gold, international securities, cash, money market funds and so on. Studies have shown that 95 percent of investment success is properly diversifying by asset class. That means that at any point in time, some parts of your investment portfolio may be going down, while others will be going up. Over the long term, you will have reduced your risk and preserved inflation-adjusted returns in your portfolio.

The second way to diversify is by specific investments within a class—having ten stocks versus just one, ten bonds versus one bond or five pieces of real estate versus one piece. This also will decrease the risk of investing while preserving the return.

The third way to diversify is by time period. As you have economic gain from your investments and you reinvest, you're diversifying by time period. You're buying into an asset class through the choice of specific investments at different times.

You don't need to be an expert investor, but you do need to ask yourself and your investment counselors, "What is our long-term strategy?" and "How are we going to diversify?"

Avoid losses. If you had $100 to invest and two choices to make, one investment guaranteed to go up 30 percent next year and the other guaranteed to go up 5 percent, which would you choose? The obvious answer is the first investment. Then assume that in the second year, the first investment declines 20 percent and the second investment again goes up 5 percent. Both investments had a net increase of 10 percent over the two-year period.

Which investment performed better? Most people, before doing the mathematics, would again choose the first investment. The mathematics, however, show that in the first case, $100 grows to $130 with a 30 percent gain, but the 20 percent loss reduces the value by $26, to $104. In the second case, the $100 had grown to slightly more than $110 in two years' time.

Thus, the return in the second case is two and a half times the return in the first case. By merely avoiding the loss and taking a small gain each year, relatively speaking, you can perform better than trying to pick the investment that will either hit a home run or strike out.

Proper diversification assumes that some of your asset classes are going to be losing value while others are increasing, but overall the portfolio is avoiding losses. That's a far wiser strategy than trying to always be in the right place at the right time.

Professional management. Another key to investment success is to realize you can't be an expert in everything. Because investing is so complex, we don't pick our own specific investments, and we recommend that others use professional managers also. That can be done through no-load mutual funds, publicly traded real estate funds, stockbrokers or others who are experts in a particular area. In chapter 14, we discuss the criteria for choosing a financial adviser.

One of the best ways to invest toward long-term goals is mutual funds. A mutual fund is, in effect, a pool of money from many investors that is entrusted to a professional manager. Mutual funds also give you diversification of your investments, total liquidity and a choice of funds to fit your specific goals.

Since funds are categorized according to their basic purpose, you need to know your investment goals. For example, long-term growth funds invest in the stocks of companies with rising earnings. Income funds invest in companies or bonds that produce high dividends. Sector funds invest in a specific industry, such as health care or gold. It's usually best to stay away from sector funds since they tend to be volatile.

Once you've picked a fund category, the chief criterion for evaluation of individual funds is performance history. Compare how funds have done over the past five years. A performance comparison for the previous nine months to one year can indicate whether funds are in tune with the market. For example, in an up market, the funds you're interested in should be up, too. Some rating services also publish a risk rating. Stay with low- to medium-risk funds, since most of them perform reasonably well even in down markets.

Beware of picking a fund simply because it's the top fund in a given year. "Hot" funds usually don't do as well next year. Consistent performance is what counts. Another caution: Past performance does not guarantee future results. Investing in stocks involves risk regardless of how you do it.

In addition to investment objectives, mutual funds also are categorized by whether there's a charge (called a load) for investing in the fund. Those that charge a fee—typically 3 to 9 percent of the amount invested—are called load funds. Those without charges are called no-load funds.

Most load funds are purchased through agents or brokers. No-load funds are available that are equal to or greater in performance than the load funds. The disadvantage to load funds is that they must go up by at least the amount of the load before you even break even. It may make sense to buy a load fund, however, if you need a broker's help to select the proper fund for your temperament and objectives.

Many periodicals evaluate the various mutual funds. As you gain information and expertise, you can switch funds..Some families of funds even allow you to switch your objectives within the same fund. It's fairly easy to determine, given your objectives, which mutual funds are appropriate for you.

When you invest in a mutual fund, you're actually buying shares of the fund (the same as you would shares of a stock). You can redeem those shares at any time; however, there may be redemption charges. Even funds without a redemption charge may impose one if you liquidate within a specified period of time after you first buy in; that's called a back-end load.

Mutual funds continue to be the best place for investing IRAs despite potential market fluctuations. Over a long period, they have provided excellent returns.

Another vehicle for use in step five is real estate investments in the form of public real estate funds, which provide diversification without the risk and liability of owning property directly. You can invest in such funds for as little as $1,000 to $5,000.

Individual investors' money is pooled in a fund typically totaling $5 million to $75 million. The money is then loaned for real estate purchases, and the fund acts as a bank, holding the first mortgages. The fund distributes to its investors their prorated shares of mortgage receipts.

Investors looking for complete safety should consider only those funds that lend money on an unleveraged basis. They can be purchased through most brokerage houses. One note of caution: Unlike the other two categories, real estate funds are for the most part nonliquid, so by definition this is a five- to ten-year investment.

Step 6: Speculating and higher-risk investments

In step six, it's important to have expert counsel in selecting additional investments. When you reach this point in the sequential investment strategy, you have significant assets and need professional tax and investment counsel before proceeding. Since your decisions will affect your taxes and cash flow, you need analyses that project into the future to determine the best investment vehicles. At this stage, the following investments become appropriate: private placement real estate offerings, oil and gas, gold and silver, first and second mortgages, professional money managers, stocks, corporate bonds, zero coupon bonds, raw land, rental property, and a host of others.

Conclusion

In concluding this book, we're mindful of several things. First, it's much easier to give advice than to practice it. Many times early in our marriage, we borrowed money to buy things we wanted. We have struggled with major spending decisions like private schools for our children, providing the right type of home, special vacations and where to invest.

Second, having been married more than twenty-five years and having most of our children raised, we've seen that time is required to solve problems, to see decisions bear fruit and to let God change you or your circumstances. In other words, don't expect to achieve financial freedom or peace of mind immediately. Just take the first step God has impressed upon you now. The second step, whatever it may be, will become apparent after the first has been taken.

God never seems to reveal His entire plan ahead of time. What He does reveal is the next step. Abraham was told to sacrifice his son Isaac. He didn't know a lamb would be provided instead, but he did know who had given the order and that He was faithful. It's the same with money management. You may not know exactly how God will lead and meet your financial needs, but by now you should know what He wants your first step to be in improving your management of the resources He provides.

We offer two thoughts in conclusion. In the parable of the talents, Jesus told of a servant who heard his master say, "Well done, good and faithful servant! You have been faithful with a few things; I will put you in charge of many things. Come and share your master's happiness!" (Matt. 25:21). Our desire is for you to stand before the Lord one day and hear Him utter those words. We want that for ourselves as well.

Second, we remind you of the promise of 1 Corinthians 1:9: "God, who has called you into fellowship with his Son Jesus Christ our Lord, is faithful." We have a friend in Jesus regardless of where we are in our financial lives, and He and His Father are faithful. We really need nothing else.

Index

If you have questions or comments about this book, Ron and Judy Blue can be reached at the following address:

Ronald Blue & Co.
1100 Johnson Ferry Road
Suite 600
Atlanta, GA 30342